Contents

Foreword vii

Acknowledgments ix

Introduction 1
    The Purpose of Journals 1
    How This Book Works 1
    Guiding Principles for Continuous Professional Learning 2

Chapter 1   **Frameworks for Change and Learning Communities** 5
    Building Learning Communities in Schools 5
    The Importance of Conversation and Building Relationships 9
    Essential Qualities and Roles of Learning Community Members 10
    Facilitating Learning Communities 11

Chapter 2   **Action Research Journal** 13
    Background of Action Research 13
    How to Use the Action Research Journal 14
    Case Study: Action Research Journal 16
    Action Research Wrap-Up 23
    Reflection and Conversation 24

Chapter 3   **Professional Growth Journal** 25
    Background of Professional Growth and Development 25
    How to Use the Professional Growth Journal 27
    Case Study: Professional Growth Journal 28
    Professional Growth Wrap-Up 38
    Reflection and Conversation 39

Chapter 4 **Staff Development Journal** 41

Background of Staff Development 41

How to Use the Staff Development Journal 41

Case Study: Staff Development Journal 43

Staff Development Wrap-Up 46

Reflection and Conversation 48

Chapter 5 **School Portfolio Journal** 49

Background of the School Portfolio 49

How to Use the School Portfolio Journal 49

Case Study: School Portfolio Journal 50

School Portfolio Wrap-Up 56

Reflection and Conversation 58

Chapter 6 **Study Group Journal** 59

Background of Study Group 59

How to Use the Study Group Journal 59

Case Study: Study Group Journal 61

Study Group Wrap-Up 65

Reflection and Conversation 66

Blacklines: **Guides and Resources** 67

Guide for Professional Collaboration 69

Banner Questions Guide 71

Professional Development Checklist 73

Professional Portfolios: Types and Purposes 74

Guide to Reflection on Professional Growth 75

Student Profile Checklist 76

Directions for Coaching Triads 77

A List of Facilitation Strategies 78

A Guide for Listening 80

Thoughtful Questions for Learning Communities 81

Worksheet for Defining Purpose and Priorities 82

School Portfolio Survey 83

A Strategy for Determining Top Priorities for School Change 84

Blacklines: Journal Forms **87**

Journal Forms for Action Research 89

Journal Forms for Professional Growth 97

Journal Forms for Staff Development 109

Journal Forms for School Portfolio 113

Journal Forms for Study Group 122

JOURNALS AS
FRAMEWORKS
for Change

Mary E. Dietz

SkyLight
Training and Publishing Inc.
Arlington Heights, Illinois

Foreword by Kay Burke

Journals as Frameworks for Change

Published by SkyLight Professional Development
2626 S. Clearbrook Dr., Arlington Heights, IL 60005-5310
800-348-4474 or 847-290-6600
Fax 847-290-6609
info@skylightedu.com
http://www.skylightedu.com

Creative Director: Robin Fogarty
Managing Editor: Ela Aktay
Acquisitions Editor: Jean Ward
Editor: Sue Schumer
Cover Design and Illustrations: David Stockman
Book Design: Donna Ramirez
Production Supervisor: Bob Crump
Proofreader: Daniel Moore
Indexer: Schroeder Indexing

LCCCN: 98-60464
ISBN 1-57517-082-5

2182B-V
Item Number 1596
Z Y X W V U T S R Q P O N M L K J I H G F E D C B
06 05 04 03 02 01 00 99   15 14 13 12 11 10 9 8 7 6 5 4 3 2

Appendix: The Learning Cycle of Professional Development 127

Glossary 135

Bibliography 139

Index 145

Foreword

"A school culture ready for improvement consists of colleagues able to share their personal values, beliefs, and visions; able to communicate and collaborate with one another to build and implement a shared vision and mission; and able to trust each other to behave in a manner consistent with a new school mission and vision." (Bernhardt 1994, 138)

The traditional methods of staff development that include top-down decision making, large-group inservices, out-of-context topics, and sometimes passive and/or resistant audiences are changing. Fueled by the report of the National Commission on Teaching and America's Future (1996) entitled *What Matters Most: Teaching for America's Future,* the one-shot "parachute drops" of workshops strategically scheduled three times a year are evolving into a more strategic type of long-term, job-embedded professional development. This emerging type of professional development empowers educators to make choices, focuses on specific student-centered goals, and fosters collaboration among peers. In addition, it encourages conversations and reflections about the teaching and learning process and, most importantly, allows educators to select the methodology that meets their individual needs as well as the needs of their students.

Many districts and states are requiring both beginning and veteran teachers to demonstrate authentic evidence of professional growth in order to receive or renew their certification. Moreover, state agencies and legislatures are moving away from traditional courses (seat time) and staff development days because they require passive listening skills rather than active involvement. More and more educators are required to use types of professional development such as peer mentoring, peer coaching, study groups, professional portfolios, action research, and reflective journals to provide authentic evidence that they are meeting their goals for improving student achievement.

Mary Dietz has been on the vanguard of this emerging form of professional development. Since 1986 she has helped teachers, administrators, school boards, and communities throughout the country begin the collaboration process that is necessary to explore and act on restructuring alternatives. Much of Mary's work with educators has been in the areas of systems design, professional development, and alternative assessments. She works at building a "community of learners" by assisting schools and school districts as well as the National Staff Development Council, the Association for Supervision and Curriculum Development, the California Staff Development Council, and the National Network for Portfolio Users.

Through her use of professional portfolios and reflective journaling, she has encouraged teachers and other members of the educational community to share thoughtful conversations about the teaching-and-learning process.

In this new book, *Journals as Frameworks for Change,* Mary explores journaling in depth by giving us the purposes and background for different types of structured journals, case studies describing where and how the tools are being implemented, and questions for reflection and conversation. In addition, she provides a wealth of resources—guides, strategies, helpful hints, and forms to effectively facilitate school communities.

This book covers the following types and purposes of structured journals:

Action Research Journal	assesses the impact of informal research on student learning
Professional Growth Journal	focuses on learning, collaboration, and assessment
Staff Development Journal	monitors the implementation process used by coaches and mentors
School Portfolio Journal	describes and reflects on various school community programs
Study Group Journal	expands and deepens understanding of a theory or practice

These types of journals can be used in isolation, but they are much more effective when they are integrated with inservices, observations, study groups, portfolios, collaborations, and other professional development activities. Journals provide authentic evidence that educators and students are making progress toward meeting their goals, outcomes, or standards. Mary Dietz skillfully demonstrates how journals serve as reflective tools and effective frameworks for facilitating educational change.

—Kay Burke
Chicago, April 1998

Acknowledgments

I would like to take this opportunity to recognize the school communities who have contributed learnings reflected in the professional journals featured in this book: The New York City Teacher Centers Consortium; Acalanes High School District, Pleasant Hill, CA; Travis Unified School District, Fairfield, CA; Round Rock Independent School District, Austin, TX; Aldine Independent School District, Houston, TX; Long Beach Unified School District, Long Beach, CA; and the California Beginning Teacher Support and Assessment programs. Through our shared experiences, we defined and refined the role of structured journals in facilitating and building capacities for learning communities.

—Mary E. Dietz

Introduction

The Purpose of Journals

Journals as Frameworks for Change is designed as a professional resource for organizing and facilitating learning communities. Structures such as action research, professional portfolio, staff development, school portfolio, and study group serve as frameworks for collaboration, learning, and—ultimately—change. Journals are essential tools designed to focus and enhance learning for professional educators as they utilize these frameworks for change and build learning communities. As educators and school community members come together, they share in a purpose and pursue deeper and broader understandings of their work. Using the structured journal process, as outlined in this book, provides opportunities for learning community participants to reflect on and consider research and new practices that will impact student learning.

Peter Senge, who pioneered the concept of the "learning community," invites educators to assist school communities in becoming "learning organizations" where they can encourage and support learning as part of their professional work (Senge 1990). If knowledge is the capacity for effective action, educators have to ask how they can facilitate learning communities to support systemic change in their schools. This book provides an answer to that question: by use of structured journals as frameworks for change.

How This Book Works

Journals as Frameworks for Change begins with a chapter on journals and learning communities, describing the role of structured journals in supporting the process of building and sustaining learning communities. Subsequent chapters offer coaching guides for using the journaling process to facilitate each type of framework for change (action research, professional portfolio, staff development, school portfolio, and study group).

Chapters begin with background on each framework and an explanation of *how* to use the structured journal to facilitate the process. See Figure 0.1 as a graphic representation of how journals can be used as frameworks for change in school communities.

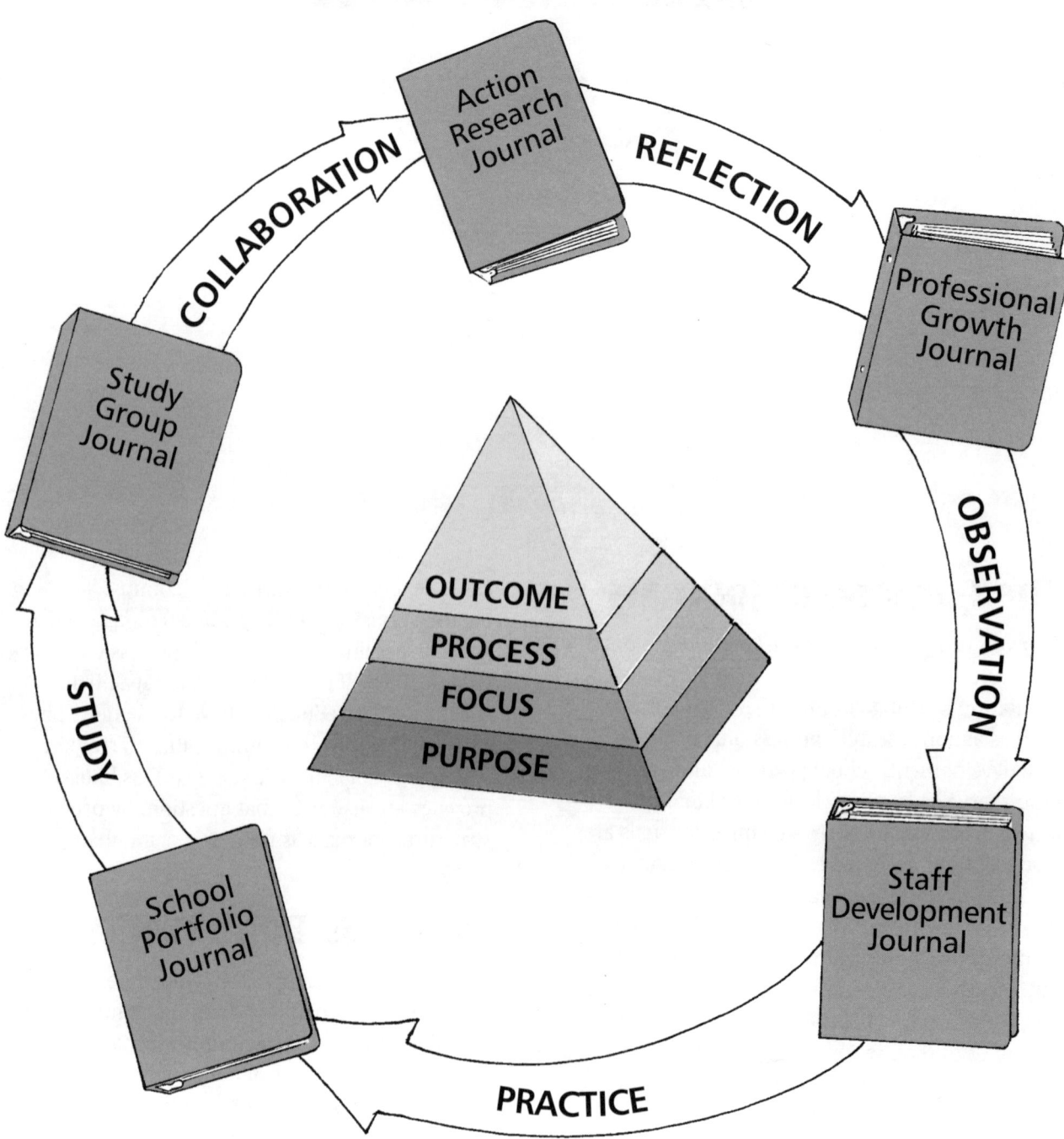

Journals as Frameworks for Change

Figure 0.1

Featured in each chapter is a Case Study and sample journal illustrating the four-step journaling process (purpose, focus, process, and outcome) that is applied for each framework for change.

The Case Study constitutes an overview of the journaling process and offers completed journal pages and activities that are drawn from actual experiences with educators and school communities across the nation. The Case Study reveals how the journaling process is applied to facilitate thoughtful reflection, observation, study, practice, and collaboration. Following the Case Study is a Wrap-Up, which summarizes how to use the structured journal for the particular framework for change. Helpful hints and strategies for implementation are included. Finally, each chapter concludes with Reflection and Conversation, a list of questions and sentence stems that provide opportunities to think about and discuss how the particular framework and journaling process can work for the individual educator and the school community.

A resource section after chapter 6 offers a wealth of forms, implementation tools, strategies, and guides that are referenced in each chapter, designed to assist learning community participants in using the structured journal process. Included are blanks for the actual journal pages (referred to as Figures) used in the chapters for each framework for change.

Journals as Frameworks for Change concludes with an appendix on the professional development learning cycle, a glossary of key terms, a bibliography that lists references and suggested readings on professional development as well as on building learning communities, and—finally—an index.

Before beginning this book and participating in the journaling process in terms of frameworks for school change, it is helpful to review the four principles on which this approach to professional learning is based. These principles form a backdrop for professional growth and collaboration as a learning community.

Guiding Principles for Continuous Professional Learning

Learning Needs to Be Learner-Centered

Professional development activities are most effective when professionals set their own goals, determine a preferred method for learning, and make decisions about how to best integrate new learnings (Krupp 1987).

Professionals Learn by Experience and Opportunities to Engage in Reflective Collaborations With Peers

Professionals will engage in learning if they are involved in the process of discovering staff development (and collegial sharing) as a structure for change. This means that professionals will be empowered to build a plan that will support their goals as well as be encouraged to question current assumptions and explore new findings, while gaining expertise and being responsible for agreed-upon outcomes (Glasser 1993).

Collaboration Supports the Restructuring of Thinking and Emergence of Staff Development

Professional growth is critical to the process of change in our schools (Joyce 1990). *Change is a process of resocialization that takes place over time and requires interaction.* Partner meetings, peer-with-peer interaction, observation, and reflection are the most effective methods for initiating substantive change (Dietz 1993).

Professionals Learn by Experience and Opportunities to Engage in Reflective Collaborations With Peers

Learning theories that apply to children have validity for adult learners as well. Using a constructivist model for teaching and being aware of the learner's readiness for change, in addition to considering where the learner is in his or her career cycle, play a vital role in the ultimate success of professional development (Brooks and Grennon-Brooks 1987).

Chapter 1

Frameworks for Change and Learning Communities

"We seek meaning and significance from building purposeful communities." (Sergiovanni 1994, xiii)

Building Learning Communities in Schools

Clusters of learning communities form a learning organization when an organization, as a whole, commits to continually learn from and about its work. Today there are many organizations that are *learning disabled,* the norms of the organization inhibiting learning from its work. For instance, a school whose professional development program is task-orientated rather than purpose-orientated forces the organization members into a narrow focus, which does not invite continuous growth.

In terms of working with learning communities in schools, there seems to be a direct relationship between success with continuous improvement efforts, and a school community in which learning is a valued part of the professional practice and conversations among staff members.

Tom Sergiovanni (1994) suggests that the desire for community is part of human nature

and a basic need. He believes that, because no cookie-cutter recipe for community building exists, each school will have to invent its own practice of community. Sergiovanni also acknowledges that, ". . . we humans seek meaning and significance above all, and building purposeful communities helps us find both."

It seems logical that having such an organization in school communities would be ideal. Educators might even assume that schools already *are* learning communities. Unfortunately, that is not the case. The lack of learning communities might even be a key contributor for the reason why so many school reform efforts have failed. In order to address the urgent needs of our educational process and define the purpose of schooling in the Information Age, an environment must be created where learning *and* constructing new ideas are an expected part of the daily practice of professional educators; a place where all can work together to challenge past practices and work toward a shared purpose, defined by professional collaboration and learning.

Is teaching a "profession"? Does it occur in an environment that invites and facilitates on-going professional practices and learning? The teaching profession is being redefined at a rapid rate by the changing needs of and purposes of education for today's youngsters and communities.

In working with the Teacher Centers in the New York City Public Schools and with other school systems, as a facilitator, I noted that educators are focused on identifying attributes of being a professional educator in the twenty-first century. The educators recognize that if their work is to support and "grow" the teaching profession in the future, they must consider the essential attributes of a professional teacher. Working with the professional development portfolio and other frameworks for change, I found the following essential attributes or mind-sets of a professional teacher emerged:

1. *Do no harm.* As a special education teacher, I interviewed students when they entered my program. I would ask, "When did you begin to believe you could not learn in school?" They could *always* tell me. They knew the circumstances, the teacher, and the event that convinced them that *"I cannot be successful here."*

As professionals, we must create a learning environment for students that encourages and nurtures whatever level of intelligence or maturity nature has provided them. We must provide a true learning environment of "coaching" all our students no matter where they are able to enter the learning process.

2. *Be an informed visionary.* So often teachers are asked to adopt another's vision or purpose of schooling. Each teacher *must* have his or her own commitment to the purpose of education, and dedication to cultivating and expanding each student's repertoire of understanding. To do this, educators must possess professional skills, know how individuals learn, know how the brain works, and know the critical juncture-points of a child's social and emotional development. With that background, professionals can add content and instructional practices that assist students in constructing their own "personal" understandings and expanding their knowledge.

3. *Inform others.* How many times have you gone to the doctor's office and really appreciated it when the doctor took the time to explain what is happening with your body, as well as the anticipated effects of a prescribed treatment? It is the same with the teaching profession. Educators need to inform themselves and their communities of the research, individual discoveries, and professional experiences that have informed and enlightened their practices. Parents always feel appreciative and more "in control" when they understand what is happening in the school environment as their children develop.

For example, there is a time in the development of a young child's visual system when reversals of letters might occur when a child is reading. Usually this lasts for a short period of time, as the brain routes and solidifies new connections. Sometimes reversal of letters is an indicator of a more complex problem, such as a perceptional disability or dyslexia. Observation and time will determine whether the exhibited phenomenon is a phase or an indicator of something else. When parents understand this, they are willing to watch and wait with the teacher, as they all observe, collaborate, and facilitate the child's developing skills.

4. Every child is unique and "unrepeatable." Educators must always remember that each child presents a new situation. Each child is unique in physical, emotional, social, and intellectual gifts and requires "customized" attention. This uniqueness celebrates and challenges professional decision making, as teachers determine the best materials and practices to

maximize learning and development for that child. This uniqueness also explains why "covering the curriculum" does not necessarily mean most students in a class have added to their knowledge base.

These four attributes share in common the need for continuous professional collaborative research and learning on the part of teachers.

The Nature of a Learning Organization and Learning Communities

A learning organization is not a building that breathes but rather a collection of community members who give life, presence, flexibility, adaptability, responsiveness, new thinking, and energy to their organization and the work it does. A learning organization is a collection of learning communities, small groups organized around individuals' work and shared purposes. The efforts of each learning community within the learning organization contribute to the co-evolving, living system (Capra 1982) which is the learning organization. The organization is dependent on learning communities to sustain it and help it grow. Learning communities infuse new thinking and suggestions for improvement into the organization, which would not exist without the collection of learning communities within the system.

Why Are Learning Communities Needed in Schools?

The breakneck speed of change in the information age has educators reeling, continually adapting and accommodating to the changing needs in our world. Learning communities allow for establishing norms of adjustment to change by continually infusing new thinking and practices into the work, accommodating changes and supporting community members through transitions. Peter Block in his book *Stewardship* commented, "If there is not transformation inside of us, all the structural change in the world will have no impact on our institutions" (Block 1993).

Learning communities invite the conversations, feedback, and risk-taking necessary for individual transformation and systemic changes. Altering a structure alone does not necessarily mean systemic change will occur.

For example, faculties in several high schools in California, going through a restructuring process, learned that block scheduling was a structural change that had little impact on student learning if teachers did not change their professional practices. The educators in the decision-making process agreed that the purpose of the block scheduling was to improve student learning by increasing the use of interactive, interdisciplinary practices. It was also agreed that block schedules could consolidate subject matter and help students focus on just a few subjects at a time, deepening their understanding of the concepts embedded in the content. Furthermore, by spending more time with fewer teachers, students would seem to have more opportunities to build a sense of community in class.

As the process for change continued, some of the school faculties chose to "vote" on whether to have block scheduling. Interestingly enough, those teachers who were forced to participate in the change to block scheduling simply did in ninety minutes what they had always done in forty-five minutes! On re-examination of those classrooms wherein the instructors were "forced" to implement block scheduling, it was found there was no change in fundamental teaching practices or student outcomes.

Another example of how changes in structures alone will not necessarily make a difference is the decision to use site-based management, as explored by a group of schools in New York. When shared decision making and site-based management (SBM) schools were considered by a group of district personnel, many of the school principals in the group seemed aligned in theory with the process, but only as long as they still had "veto" power over decisions. However, teachers who came to the table as part of the process were very much interested in decision-making power regarding hirings and budget allocations. So there was a roomful of people who were negotiating for shared governance. The conversations were not about how student learning could be improved, but about power. Participants were operating off an old paradigm, and altering the structure did nothing to alter the conditions.

Over time, however, the conversations began to evolve into asking about purpose and how site-based management could help achieve that purpose. The team facilitators began asking questions: What do we need to know about shared decision making? What do *we* want for *our* school? As team members became willing to listen and learn, they began building their understandings and abilities, resulting in a change in their attitudes toward the process, thus contributing toward a shared purpose as a school community. Through the process of questioning, individuals had shifted their power and purpose; change was actually achieved in a meaningful way.

Members of the Learning Community Working Toward Change

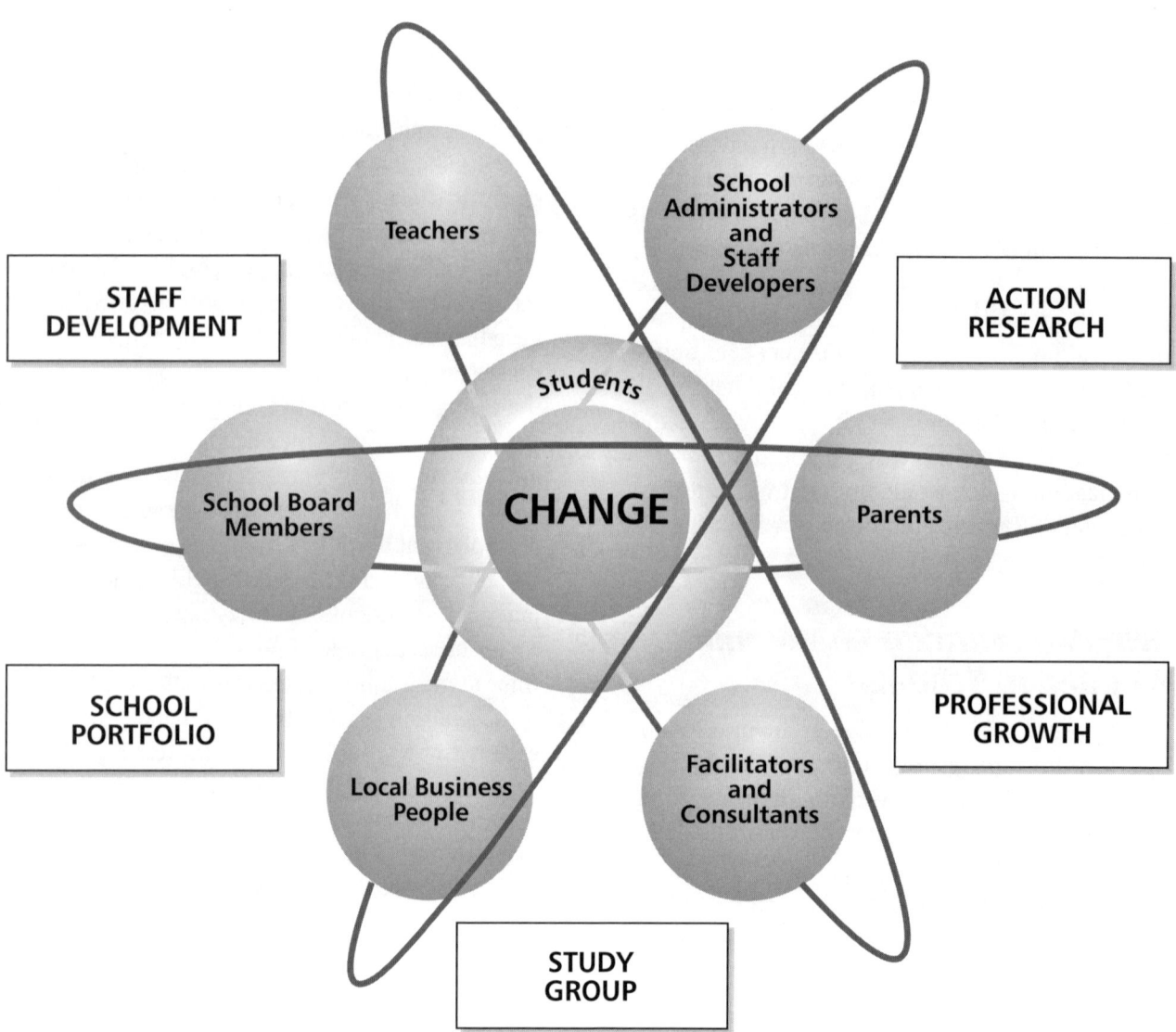

Figure 1.1

Who Is in a Learning Community?

Members of a learning community are individuals with *diverse* philosophies, experiences, expertise, and personalities. Within a school community, learning communities can and do include members inside and outside the walls of the school building, as shown in Figure 1.1. The community-at-large is responsible for the educational process of youngsters; therefore, building learning communities composed of all parties involved in the educational process is critical. Professional educators come to their work with varying values, skills, knowledge bases, and beliefs. Their first and foremost challenge is to align their needs and purposes with those of the entire community. All learning community members are part of the critical life force of the organization. Their collaborations, interactions, and shared understandings are the life force that energizes and connects individuals and forms cohesive learning communities. Through working together, the individuals recognize their interdependence and the richness in their diversity. Learning communities in schools should include children, educators, parents, business partners, and other organizations in the community which contribute to the schooling process.

One school in southern California was experiencing great divisiveness among staff and community. The community was demanding changes in the school, focusing on staff development practices and the lack of equity in the bussing process. The conversations in parent group meetings became heated and, at times, ugly. The school leadership decided to have a community night and redesign the process of using parent opinions and desires in the decision-making process at the school.

The first step in the process was to reconstruct the history of the school. Community members were invited to join the staff for an evening to tell the "story" of their school. They recounted changes that had occurred in curriculum, staff, student enrollment, assessments, and physical structures. Working in decade groups, the participants recounted the history of the school from the decade in which it opened to the 1990s. After a representative from each group summarized the highlights of that particular decade, everyone looked for outstanding achievements in which they felt pride. Group participants then discussed what to "keep" and the lessons that had been learned.

Drawing from the experience of that evening, the group began to set a new purpose and priorities for the school. For each priority they formed an action team, which included a school staff member. Community members were invited to participate on a team that addressed one of their greatest interests or concerns. Several staff members and parents attended facilitation training sessions and were willing to serve as team facilitators. The action teams met monthly and developed a plan with both short- and long-term goals. The first "community night" meeting was in 1994 and, to this day, the learning community process established that night still serves that school community as they work together to address the challenge of educating children.

The Importance of Conversation and Building Relationships

Building relationships is at the heart of learning communities. The reciprocal process of *co-learning* fuels the continued growth and vitality within the community. Members of a learning community are committed to continually improving their efforts and refining their practices on an on-going basis. They are willing and able to move out of isolation and engage in collegial (professional) conversations about their work.

School communities as well as communities at-large are experiencing complex problems that are not easily resolved. These problems have been referred to as falling into one of two categories, wicked problems and tame problems. Wicked problems are complex and not easily definable. There are no existing algorithms for solving wicked problems, and they are iterative in nature; that is, the problems are recursive and continually evolving. Tame problems, on the other hand, are definable. The boundaries of involvement and areas for intervention appear clear. There are existing algorithms. Today schools and communities are facing greater numbers of wicked problems that are not effectively solved with an easy answer. These are problems that are multidimensional, self-generating, and that require continual attention and adaptations (Bailey 1996).

Members of learning communities put meaning into their work by defining a common purpose and function. The emphasis in a learning community is on building commitment, not on constructing compliant structures. The environment is one of shared responsibility rather than managerial accountability. In these times of wicked problems, there is an increased need to work together and to be open to new ideas and new solutions. When solutions are mandated solutions, forced upon the organization from the outside, there is little possibility for building commitment for implementation of shared solutions, nor for willingness to continually revisit the effectiveness of the mandated solution over time.

Essential Qualities and Roles of Learning Community Members

In a learning community, individual members are both *learners* and *leaders* who are willing to suspend assumptions, respect the ideas of others, and engage in dialogue to continually construct and refine their purpose and shared understandings. As members take responsibility for learning and leading together, they build new understandings of leadership and leadership actions. Learning community members are *adaptive, generative,* and *creative* with their practices. They

are committed to continually improving their work by engaging in reflective collaborations. They seek new ideas, feedback, and opportunities to reflect and collaborate. Members are leaders who take action to generate new thinking and construct new designs for their work.

Each individual member is an integral part of a dynamic, evolving system. The system as a whole is greater than the sum of the parts. Synergy exists. In a learning community there is recognition of members' interdependence and a reciprocal process of learning. Each member is committed to infusing new ideas, rethinking existing structures, and reflecting on experiences. As members interact (with people, events, and ideas) and reflect on their experiences, each person contributes to the evolving process of the learning community and its members.

Members of learning communities establish trusting relationships by clearly articulating intentions and purposes. Relationships are formed with respect, honesty, and professional ethics. Collegiality builds among members as they clarify their intentions and identify assumptions to avoid misunderstandings. Members recognize how the flow of information and the dynamics of learning are disrupted when faulty assumptions are made regarding intentions.

Learning communities invite the whole person. Community members nourish and enhance the on-going cognitive, experiential, and emotional development of learning community members (Dietz 1994). This happens through the interactions, trust-building, and hard work aimed toward a shared purpose. Structures or frameworks such as action research and study groups offer "openings" to build relationships that invite shared learning.

On-going relationships generate energy and cohesiveness in order to facilitate and sustain the learning system's communities. Margaret Wheatley states that relationships are key in supporting systemic change. She points out ". . . that we do not really know who we are until we enter into a relationship with another" (Wheatley 1992, 44). It's only during the relationship-building stage that people are challenged to define who they are, what they do, and their contribution to an organization.

Learning communities are formed one conversation at a time, through reflection and interaction with others about their experiences, ideas, and purposes. Members increase their capacity to listen, to dialogue, and to construct new understandings. Increased trust and knowledge of shared purpose enable members to make decisions for the good of the learning community, which in turn serves the good of individuals. Members recognize the ultimate benefits of finding common ground, and respect each other's contribution to achievements.

Members of learning communities work toward agreement of both purpose and actions to fulfill that purpose. Each member assumes leadership roles and takes leadership actions as appropriate (Lambert et al. 1995). Learning communities need members who

- Facilitate conversations and decision making.
- Acknowledge the history, norms, and pride in the organization.
- Support members through the disequilibrium of change.
- Accept responsibility for the learning of self and of others in the organization.

Members of learning communities learn from their work and from each other. They welcome opportunities to invent meaningful and purposeful staff development experiences and continually refine their practice. Accepting their responsibility to stay informed about new practices and research that applies to their work, learning community members are mindful of their commitment to improve continually, and support each other in redesigning and modifying their professional behaviors.

Facilitating Learning Communities

"Learning communities are groups of individuals who have come together with a shared purpose and agree to construct new understandings . . . a place where people continually expand their capacity to create the results they truly desire, where new and expansive patterns of thinking are nurtured, where collective aspiration is set free, and where people are continually learning how to learn together."
(Senge 1990, 14).

Building a sense of community within a group, a learning community starts with relationships and evolves one conversation at a time. Relationships grow when there is a framework or structure for conversation, work, and reflection; when there is a commitment to building the capacity to have meaningful, focused conversations; and when there is a recognition and commitment on the part of members. Building relationships is a critical factor that influences the impact of the group members' learnings on their professional work.

Frameworks for change, and the use of the journal process within those frameworks, are helpful in supporting and sustaining learning communities. Following are three examples of how people working together in learning communities can achieve school improvement through such frameworks:

Action research: A group of first grade teachers study assessment strategies and use their classrooms to evaluate which system will help them best demonstrate student growth for parents.

Study groups: A group of school leaders decide to meet several times during the school year to read and review a guide on assessment in learning organizations, in order to determine some authentic applications that could positively change the assessment process in their schools.

Program quality review: A school's teaching staff makes a commitment to review new assessment methods for measuring the impact of their classroom practices on student learning. They agree to generate essential questions and pursue an inquiry process, which leads them to understanding the gaps in their programs and identifying action priorities for change.

Members of learning communities build capacity by developing knowledge, skills, and attitudes that will help them grow professionally. Professional development is achieved through experiences with constructivist leadership, knowledge of adult learning, and awareness of constructivist learning theory. Drawn from an understanding of systems, communication abilities, and acceptance of the dynamics of change, facilitation skills are essential to focus and organize a learning community.

Attitudes and attributes that support learning communities include

- Respect for diversity of others and willingness to suspend assumptions.
- Honor of another's history and respect of cultural norms.
- Willingness to seek understanding of others' intentions.
- Willingness to listen and learn.
- Openness to posing and responding to essential questions.
- Recognition of the vital role of learning communities.
- Acceptance that certainty is a myth.
- Commitment to making learning communities a priority.

Many school systems around the world have begun to assess the "condition" of their school communities. Teachers within those systems and other school community members, seeking to establish themselves as learning organizations, are looking for a way to begin the process of change—an "entry point." The vision of transforming schools into learning organizations provides a cohesive and agile framework for educators entering the twenty-first century. As a result of this vision, there is a new paradigm for schools: learner-centered instruction, purposeful learning, and continual improvement of professional practices.

Chapter 2

Action Research Journal

"The most superb effect of cooperative action research is synergy, in which products of collective thought and problem solving are greater than the sum of efforts of each individual working alone." (Schmuck 1997, ix)

Background of Action Research

An example of a structure or framework for building learning communities is *action research*. Action research involves focused, systematic inquiry, and data collection in search of new understandings regarding an issue, question, problem, or dilemma. During the early decades of the twentieth century, educational philosopher John Dewey wrote about reflection and action as part of an educator's work. Since that time, many forms of research have developed in the teaching profession. As we enter the twenty-first century, the teacher as researcher, engaging in action research, holds great promise for creating learning communities.

For teacher-researchers in school settings, questions of practice focus the action research. These questions can occur at the classroom level, or they can be drawn from dilemmas and reflections of thoughtful teachers on a daily basis.

Action research and inquiry conducted by a group or community of learners can have a significant impact on teaching practices. This direct connection between inquiry and action is the power in teacher as researcher. The people who *do* the work, know best how to *improve* the work. When communities of professional educators come together to research their work, they are in the best position to make direct changes in their teaching practices.

Action research is a powerful learning opportunity for teachers. In the collaborative form of action research, teachers work together to define problems for study and conduct the investigation once the question or problem is defined. Sometimes teachers will examine various aspects of the same problem and contribute their data and analysis to the larger goal. In other situations, teachers will work together on the same problem, analyzing the same evidence and capitalizing on the different perspectives the researchers bring to the table.

Communities of teacher-researchers are common now in many parts of the United States. As an example, as of the late 1990s in California a growing number of teacher-researcher groups have been forming in an effort to study the impact of class-size reduction on student learning. Many of the primary level classes in California have been reduced to twenty or fewer students. The teachers involved in this change immediately "felt" a difference. Those participating in action research groups related to this particular study are dedicated to identifying the indicators of student success in their classrooms as a result of lowering the class size. They have been eager to study and document the impact on student learning, seeking to preserve and expand "rightsizing" of classes for the future.

Through action research, teachers become confident about their work, more knowledgeable about school change, more likely to assume leadership roles, better able to communicate with colleagues, and more knowledgeable about the role of learning in teaching (Richert 1994).

There are many features of action research as a process that underscore the role of learning. In the action research process, teachers examine questions that are important to them. As they draw from their experience the questions that matter to them most, teachers become more aware of themselves as definers and constructors of knowledge, and realize the power of their ideas. The journal process presented in this chapter serves as a guide to facilitate and "coach" action research as a framework for change.

How to Use the Action Research Journal

Clarifying the purpose and function of collegial collaboration is first and foremost in terms of any framework for change, including action research. A useful strategy for the group members at this beginning point is considering what professional collaboration means to them, and what experiences they have had with it in the past. To orientate members and establish ground rules, the group may use questions such as the following:

- How have we previously worked together?

- Are we just getting to know each other?

- How would we like this group to function?

As the participants reflect, talk, and listen in an effort to establish a shared purpose and function for their learning community, they will naturally get acquainted and begin to build relationships.

Organization

Learning communities are built on the capacity to collaborate and the commitment to listen, learn, and ask questions. The structured journal gives the members of the group a "container" or guidelines for initiating their action research by using the following goals or organizers:

- Establish a *purpose*. Why are we forming our group? What is our overarching purpose and our desired outcome?

- *Focus* the inquiry. What are the specific issues or dilemmas we hope to "research"?

- Design a *process*. How will we pursue our inquiry? What activities will we engage in? What data will we collect? When will we meet to share findings and how will we collaborate? What are the time lines? What is our plan?

- Set an *outcome*. How will we share our collection of data and our reflections to conclude and summarize our findings?

Action research supports teacher-researchers as they identify specific challenges within their classroom and research by planning, acting, reflecting, and revising. The four organizers of the journal process (purpose, focus, process, and outcome) contribute to a phase of the research process. Following is a model outline that reflects those organizers and shows the design of the structured journal as it applies to the action research process:

I. Introduction

II. Purpose

    A. Observations

III. Focus

    A. Research Target Area

IV. Process

    A. Plan

    B. Act

    C. Refine

V. Outcome

    A. Reflections

Activities at each step guide the group participants in directing their action research inquiry as they collect data, observe learning, and refine practices.

Journal Design and Process

Purpose, focus, process, and outcome are key components in the action research journal process. The following is a template for the process, denoting the actions and questions for reflection that characterize each component:

Why? (Purpose)

OBSERVATIONS • CONCERNS • QUESTIONS

- Why do we want to form this action research group?
- How long will we work together?
- How will we collaborate and take action on learnings?

What If? (Focus)

ESTABLISHING A RESEARCH TARGET AREA

- What do we need to know?
- What are we especially interested in?
- What do we wonder about?
- What are some of our concerns?

How Will It Work? (Process)

PLAN • DATA COLLECTION • COLLABORATION

- When will we meet?
- How will we collect data?
- What process will we use for observations and information gathering?
- How will we share roles and responsibilities in the group?

So What? (Outcome)

OBSERVATIONS • LEARNINGS • REFINEMENTS • ACTIONS

- How has our research impacted our work?
- How will we communicate findings?
- What actions will we take?

The action research journal consists of the following actions as participants carry out the steps of purpose, focus, process, and outcome:

- Participate in the initial purpose-setting process for action research.
- Establish the target area for research.
- Identify a collaboration network to support and enhance inquiry.
- Collect information, strategies, skills, and materials related to the targeted research area.
- Plan; design a plan to study target area.
- Act; implement plan and assess impact.
- Reflect and revise; engage in reflective collaborations and describe the outcome.
- Consider making adaptations as indicated by research findings.
- Assess the effectiveness of the action research process.

The action research journal can serve as a tool to focus and direct conversations and research activities, as well as to assist with drawing conclusions about research findings. The process can bring participants together around a common purpose, such as how to deal with a key decision or with a dilemma the school is facing. When working with a group of educators and other learning community members, a facilitator can assess their readiness regarding collaboration by asking questions such as:

- Have we worked together before?

- Are we accustomed to listening and questioning in active dialogues with each other?

If the participants lack a shared history of working together in a collaborative way, the facilitator might want to begin with activities and discussions that build community (shared understanding and beliefs). These preliminary conversations will build a foundation for the group to clarify their purpose and desired outcome in terms of the action research process.

Refer to the blacklines section of this book for the following helpful tools to use during this process: Guide for Collaboration (page 69) and Guide for Listening (page 80).

Case Study: Action Research Journal

Following is an overview of the journaling process, including samples of journals and activities from actual action research experiences within a school community. On the journal pages in this section, participants' responses are set in italics so that the various types of notes and reflections that are prompted by the journaling process can be easily identified. Commentary is provided before each form, explaining how the group under study applied the journaling process to facilitate action research as a framework for school change.

Why? (Purpose)

OBSERVATIONS • CONCERNS • QUESTIONS

- Why do you want to form this action research group?
- How long will you work together?
- How will you collaborate and take action on learnings?

The action research journal provides a framework for identifying, planning, and facilitating research. It provides opportunities for

1. Identifying a target area for research.
2. Building a research plan.
3. Collecting information.
4. Collaborating with peers as research partners.
5. Observing.
6. Assessing impact of strategies used in target area.
7. Refining practices.
8. Reflecting on experiences.

Purpose Statement . . .
The purpose of our action research team is to determine the impact of class size on student learning. Now that we have reduced our first-grade classes to twenty students (previously thirty-three students), we anticipate there will be greater opportunities for individualized instruction and that student learning will improve. We hope to PROVE the impact on student learning and to document the shift in our instructional practices.

Figure 2.1 Sample Purpose

When you, as a facilitator or member of a learning community, are ready to apply the journaling process, note that blanks of the journal forms for action research shown here are offered in the blacklines section (see pages 89–96).

The questions at the top of the first journal form, Figure 2.1, regard the purpose and serve as organizers for discussions about why the group is forming, what the participants' beliefs and concerns are, and how the group will schedule meetings.

At this point, the group participants orientate themselves to the action research journal design and begin the first step of the process, establishing purpose.

Using an observation form (see Figure 2.2), group participants reflect on their observations about current practices and student learning.

Observations

1. What are your observations regarding student learning?

   Since we have lowered the class size, I am noticing subtle differences in how some students listen, follow directions, and are aware of communications in the classroom. I am able to move the class through activities in less time and it seems to take less practice for them to establish routines in class.

2. Describe strategies and practices that have been effective and others that have not worked so well.

   I have been trying to decide on an effective way to implement learning centers. One of our goals in the class-size reduction process is to schedule more individualized instructional time and to apply a diagnostic teaching model. I have been trying to identify appropriate independent tasks for students to do at the centers.

3. What are your interests and concerns about your work?

   I realize there is a need to document student learning and to provide data and dialogues that reflect improvement in student learning. My greatest concern is that we might be asking for results that are developmentally inappropriate. I am concerned that we might begin to establish inappropriate expectations of young students.

Figure 2.2 Sample Observations

The next step of the journaling process is Focus (see Figure 2.3). The group participants reflect on the banner questions, the key questions that will drive their inquiry and work.

At this point, discussions lead to focusing—identifying a specific area for action research and inquiry. The banner questions are used to facilitate discussion and identify the "target" for research.

What If? (Focus)

BANNER QUESTIONS

- What do you need to know?
- What are you especially interested in?
- What do you wonder about?
- What are some of your concerns?

Research Team Establishes a Research Target

We as researchers reflect on observations and learnings from teaching experiences and pose questions. These questions represent puzzling experiences such as, "How can I determine readiness to begin reading with such diversity among my first grade class?" "I wonder why." These observations and questions will help us build a pathway for identifying strategies and employing innovative practices to research and study the connections among theories, practice, and students' learning.

Research Focus Discussion

Our group has brainstormed all of our concerns and interests regarding class-size reduction and how to best focus our research. We have decided to focus on the development of literacy abilities. We will collect data that will help us trace student development and learning in the area of literacy and reading, in particular.

Figure 2.3 Sample Focus

Research Target

What is the impact of class-size reduction on student learning in the area of literacy development and reading in particular?

I. Action Questions

What if . . .

We all used the same inventory materials to assess student growth?

How about . . .

Working together to align our instructional materials and practices in the first grade classrooms?

(continued on next page)

How could I . . .

Document and reflect on my observations and changes in my practices as a result of smaller class size?

II. Collegial Connections

What practices and models have others used?

Are my colleagues having similar experiences?

III. Strategies and Skills to Implement

Our goal is . . .

To complete literacy system within our school.

We need to address . . .

How we will select assessment materials to document growth.

How the system will work.

How we will work together to standardize the assessment process among our first-grade team members.

Figure 2.4 Sample Research Target

The participants use the Research Target form (see Figure 2.4) to guide discussions. Lead-ins or sentence stems are instrumental to reflection in the action research journal process.

Having determined the research target, the participants move to the Process step of the journal. Using the questions in the Process form (see Figure 2.5), the participants determine their plan, their method(s) of data collection, and their methods of collaboration. A facilitator may use the Guide for Professional Collaboration on pages 69–70 in the blacklines section.

How Will It Work? (Process)

PLAN • DATA COLLECTION • COLLABORATION

- When will you meet?
- How will you collect data?
- What process will you use for observations and information gathering?
- How will you share roles and responsibilities in the group?

PLAN • ACT • REFLECT • REVISE
Research Plan

- Strategies to be employed
- Implementation plan
- Data collection template
- Observations and reflective collaborations
- Refinements of the plan

Figure 2.5 Sample Process

Next, using the Research Plan Strategy form (see Figure 2.6), participants determine their plan of action, the preparation needed, and the schedule for implementation.

The challenge in the process is to use the structured journal effectively to organize and guide a plan and strategy for research. If the participants have clearly agreed on a purpose and have identified a research target, they should be able to generate action questions that focus specifically on what they—as a learning community—want to learn from the actions they take and the data they collect.

Research Plan (Strategy)

We will meet as a grade level once every two weeks to share findings and observations, and to refine process. We will begin with identifying critical literacy areas to assess for first graders to establish a base line for study. Where are the students in terms of their development and abilities? We will assess letter recognition, sound/ symbol relationship (long and short vowels), as well as word recognition, fluency, and listening comprehension.

Preparation

Materials: *What assessment materials will we use?*

Methods: *How will we practice and observe the assessment process with each other? How will we collect data?*

Resources: *What will our needs be in terms of materials and release time? What is available to us? In what areas would we like staff development?*

Implementation Schedule

August	*Area meeting for establishing purpose and action targets.*
September	*Developmental literacy discussion.* *Assessment planning for literacy.*
October	*Begin baseline data collection.*
November	*Share assessment findings and study literacy profiles of students.*
December	*Explore literacy staff development that aligns with students' needs from assessments.*
January	*Plan for mid-year assessments.*
February	*Discuss staff developments and practices used by team members, what is working, and what we want to know more about.*
March	*Collect data from fall and mid-year assessments and reflect on findings; discuss connections to staff development design.*
May	*Collect final assessment data.*
June	*Draw conclusions from student growth patterns and instructional practices; make recommendations for continued study next term.*

Figure 2.6 Sample Research Plan (Strategy)

Using the Data Collection Form (see Figure 2.7), the group—having established what data they need to collect—endeavors to keep the data collection system as simple as possible. As teacher-researchers, group participants realize that data collection is a critical step in the action research process.

It is important to remember that *what* data are collected and *how* the data are collected will determine the validity of the action research, particularly when conclusions are drawn. The data collection system in the action research process should not be so complex that it interferes with regular routines or makes the data less meaningful.

Data Collection Form

Collecting and Analyzing Multiple Sources of Data to Study the Impact of Action Plans

WHO (demographic data to be collected)

Number of Students:

Gender: M _____   F _____

Stable student population (over 3 years):

Attendance:

Other:

HOW (processing of data and strategies in research plan)

Focusing on events that are happening and things we are doing related to our target action area. For example, do collections of numbers to chart frequency and seek patterns. Since the target area is writing and we are trying new writing strategies, collect some of the following data:

Students are writing (x) times a week.

We are meeting in writing groups (x) times monthly.

SO WHAT (outcomes—formal and informal data)

Assessment:

Formal and/or traditional testing.

Alternative assessment.

Feedback and observations.

Other Outcomes

Impacts expected and unexpected from action plan.

Surveys

Comments from students.

Figure 2.7 Sample Data Collection Form

The final session for the group is devoted to the Outcome step of the process (see Figure 2.8), with each group participant drawing conclusions, speaking as an individual and as a group member, and making suggestions for change based on the group's action research.

To close the action research journal process, the group celebrates their accomplishments as a learning community and considers identifying steps for further inquiry. A facilitator may use the following tool in the blacklines section for this purpose: Thoughtful Questions for Learning Communities (page 81).

So What? (Outcome)

OBSERVATIONS, LEARNINGS, REFINEMENTS, ACTIONS

- How has your research impacted your work as an educator?
- How will you communicate findings?
- What actions will you take?

CONCLUSIONS, REFLECTIONS, RETHINKING, AND LEARNINGS

As a result of working in our action research team, I realized the power of collaboration and how much I was able to learn from my colleagues. We have been doing a lot of the same things and experiencing many similar problems, and yet we never had an opportunity to discuss them.

We have just begun to clarify our purpose for the long term. Probably we had very high expectations for ourselves when we began, trying to do too much in one year. We did learn that the diagnostic model is very helpful for understanding children's development of literacy abilities. Continuing our conversation about what is a balanced, individualized literacy staff development will be very important.

Has the class-size reduction made a difference with student learning? Yes! We have been better able to focus on multiple aspects of the developing literacy process and to customize, assess, and support the development process. Next year, if we continue to collect and share data for each of our students, I am sure we will see the overall differences with end-of-the-term achievement levels as compared to the number of students with delayed learning problems entering second grade in the past .

I observed the effectiveness of learning centers in my class with smaller class size. I was better able to identify students' independent levels for working at the centers and to prepare students for participating in the routine of "center time." There was virtually no wasted time addressing problems at the centers while I was conducting individual reading conferences.

What hypotheses did you bring to your research target area?
I thought class-size reduction would make my job easier, I also thought that students would learn at a faster rate with individual attention. Both of these seemed to be validated by our data collections and collegial sharing.

How did the data collection support your learning?
The data collection helped me target key areas of literacy development and have specific information to customize a literacy staff development for each student. The data collection also helped in our discussions about the most effective practices and materials.

What new questions have emerged from your research?
I would like to continue to study, along with my group, the long-term impact of class-size reduction and how we can better capitalize on our use of time and resources. I would like to address how we can share data with parents and gain confidence in the community support for smaller class size.

Figure 2.8 Sample Outcome

Action Research Wrap-Up

Action research is a powerful process for focusing on inquiry and data collection. As revealed in the previous Case Study, working as an individual as well as with colleagues—as part of a learning community—is key to the process.

Selecting a research target area that is integral to your professional work has everything to do with a successful action research journal experience. That way, your work as a teacher-researcher will not be considered an add-on to your regularly scheduled duties.

Furthermore, you, as part of a learning community, will have a process for reflecting, collaborating, and learning from your daily interactions in class. As a result of action research, you and your group will have new information to *inform* and *improve* teaching practices throughout the school community, as well as work meaningfully toward school change.

Using the structured journal as a guide, you

- Establish a *purpose* for your research.
- Identify a *focus,* a research target.
- Design a *plan* and *process* for research.
- Move your plan into *action.*
- Reflect on the *outcome.*
- *Revise* practices and work toward change, as indicated by research.

Helpful Hints

Having a container for your research data and notes—your collection of artifacts, evidence, and so on—helps! Consider a zipper bag, a roomy canvas bag, or a file box filled with folders.

Reflection and Conversation

Identifying Opportunities for Using Action Research

1.   I would like to understand why my students seem to consistently have difficulty with . . .

2.   What studies have been completed that deal with . . .

3.   What would the impact on student learning be if I were to . . .

4.   We could incorporate action research efforts with our teacher evaluation system by . . .

5.   The benefits of having an action research team are . . .

6.   How should we schedule time to meet and reflect on our learnings?

Chapter 3

Professional Growth Journal

"Continuous development of all teachers is the cornerstone for meaning, improvement and reform. Professional development and school development are intrinsically linked." (Fullan 1991, 315)

Background of Professional Growth and Development

A valuable framework for change, professional growth—specifially in terms of the portfolio—is a process that supports teacher learning and contributes to establishing new norms for professional development and evaluation. My work with professional growth and portfolio design began in 1987 while working with Mariam True at the Professional Development Consortium in San Diego, where we clarified the connection between professional growth and the use of journaling to sustain a learner-centered process. In the Consortium's pilot project in the late 1980s, teachers successfully used the learner portfolio framework, a portfolio structure and process that was not only teacher-directed and supported by peer collaboration, but endorsed by the school administration.

A history of the development of the professional portfolio has to include the benchmark work reported by Kenneth Wolf in a 1991 *Kappan* article. Using the portfolio as a collection of items, such as a presentation portfolio for exhibiting and/or recording professional accomplishments of teachers, was the subject of that article, with a focus on the TAP, the Teacher Assessment Project at Stanford done in collaboration with Lee Schulman (Wolf 1991).

Wolf reported that, while the TAP project was intended to assist with the design and plans for the National Board of Teaching Standards, it ultimately led to the notion of the *working portfolio* as teacher evaluation. The portfolio approach envisioned by the TAP project was one in which others direct the nature of and the process by which the artifacts and evidence are collected and exhibited by the learner (the teacher).

In February 1989, however, Christopher Clark of Michigan State University introduced a completely different course of action as he presented a paper on professional growth at the International Conference on Teacher Development. In his presentation, he described *self-directed* professional development of teachers—an approach quite different from the "evaluation by others" approach exemplified by the TAP project. Clark's plan did not mention using a portfolio, but it did recommend a design for teachers to self-assess and reflect on their practices. Addressing an important turning point for professional growth, Clark analyzed the research on "teacher thinking" and the teacher-as-learner approach (reflection and collaboration as opposed to evaluation by others), a movement that had begun back in 1976.

Today this framework of professional growth is viewed as a valuable tool, a structure to focus and facilitate growth in professional practices. The focus for learning, the *essential question* for inquiry, is learner-generated and aimed at connecting the needs and interests of individuals with their work and the purpose of schooling in their school community. As I first envisioned it in a 1989 study (Dietz 1993), the educator's professional portfolio is designed today around four steps to be taken by the learner (the individual teacher):

- *Purpose*—Asking why you are "doing" a professional portfolio.

- *Focus*—Asking what your theme for professional learning will be.

- *Process*—Asking how and with whom you will collaborate, learn, and reflect.

- *Outcome*—Asking what you will learn and what you want to do next.

This portfolio process, specifically tailored to the professional portfolio as a framework for school change, has led to revising the evaluation process for educators nationwide. My work with the professional portfolio as a framework for change began with teachers at Central Union High School in El Centro, California, in 1989, and with the staff at Orange County Public Schools in Orlando, Florida, in 1992. After its introduction to

the public schools in Orange County, Florida, in 1994, the professional portfolio process outlined in this chapter was adopted countywide as part of the teacher assessment system. The NYC (New York City) Teacher Center Consortium completed their pilot study on the professional portfolio in 1995; currently, the portfolio is an alternative assessment option for teachers in the New York City public schools.

Often, professional portfolios are viewed—at least initially—as a collection of "things" to be reviewed and, in some cases, evaluated by another individual without the learner (the creator of the portfolio) being present. However, the portfolio concept as presented in this text is more about the professional portfolio as an organizer or process for deepening the levels of understandings, exploration, and assimilation of new thinking about teaching and learning practices. As such, the portfolio is not created or evaluated in isolation; it is not measured by a simple rubric; and, since it is a process rather than a collection of "things," it is not viewed as being consumable.

Portfolios that have gone in that single dimension, as a collection rather than a process, have lost the dynamics of inquiry, collaboration, and reflection for learning. This is a significant loss, since the mission of teachers today is to become self-directed and assert leadership actions. Journaling as part of the portfolio process offers role flexibility, dialogue, reflection, conversation, and collaboration, allowing educators to fulfill their mission in terms of professional growth. The portfolio process is reciprocal, not hierarchical, inviting uncertainty as well as thoughtful reconsideration and restructuring.

Many school districts across the nation have made the commitment to build true learning communities for teachers, and have successfully used the portfolio as a means of professional growth. Often using a combination of professional portfolio types, many of these school communities have designed a process that truly facilitates professional development.

A derivation of the professional portfolio process is the school portfolio, a portfolio that represents the work, the focus, and the outcome of schoolwide performance as well as change efforts. The process of collecting, selecting, and reflecting on artifacts and evidence (data that represent the evolution as well as the purpose of education in that particular school system) contributes to the emergence of the school's voice in the community. Reflections that accompany the school portfolio tell the "story" about the school, its purpose, and its growth and role in the community. The journaling process in terms of the school portfolio is covered in-depth in chapter 5.

Many positive results have occurred as a result of offering the professional portfolio as a learning opportunity (an opportunity for professional growth) to teachers. In the early 1990s, Dr. Sharon Graves at the University of Ohio, Dayton, conducted a four-year case study on the implementation of the portfolio process in schools, and reported the following findings (Graves 1996):

- Teachers found the "professional development portfolio" to be an excellent framework to gain focus on their personal and professional growth.

- Portfolio development stages were different for each participant.

- Once it was established that teachers would have control over their own professional growth, they needed time to adjust to the change.

- After having engaged in the professional portfolio process, teachers no longer felt the need to refer to a prescribed organization; they had internalized the process.

- Learning to self-assess involved time, feedback, and reflection on the part of teachers.

These benefits and changes represent an important opportunity for educators to take charge of their professional development and learning.

How to Use the Professional Growth Journal

"Those who dare to teach must never cease to learn."—Socrates

The professional growth journal, as part of professional development and the portfolio process, can be used to organize and focus collaborations among teachers who have the option of participating in the portfolio process, either in place of or as part of professional evaluation. The portfolio process is designed to focus and facilitate learning, with the context (topic) and nature of artifacts and evidence gathered as part of the portfolio being determined by the teacher acting as a learner. Therefore, the professional portfolio is a learner-centered portfolio. With that in mind, as the professional portfolio process is implemented, it is best to begin with an overview of the process, along with a discussion regarding the shared purpose for participation as well as the "boundary conditions" of evaluation.

To establish the conditions at the outset, it is helpful for participants to ask the following questions:

- Who will be looking at the portfolio artifacts and evidence?

- Will the end result of the process be a professional development portfolio? Will it be used as part of the learner's professional evaluation?

- If the portfolio is part of the evaluation process, will the evaluator participate in roundtable discussion groups when the teacher group(s) meet to discuss learnings and explore opportunities to collaborate?

- What will the outcome requirements be if the portfolio process is part of teacher evaluations?

Next, participants orientate themselves as to how the professional growth journal process, used within the framework of the portfolio, serves as a guide for reflections and collaborations. The critical steps in implementing the journaling process are: establishing a shared purpose, identifying a banner question (the "big question" for the inquiry/journaling/portfolio process), and committing to several "checkpoint" meetings. A checkpoint meeting is essentially a periodic roundtable discussion about participant work, observations, learnings, and questions that have emerged during the journaling or portfolio process.

Organization

Following is a model outline for the professional growth journal, reflecting the organizers of the process:

I. Purpose
   A. Credo

II. Focus
   A. Banner Question

III. Process
   A. Professional Development Plan
   B. Artifacts and Evidence

IV. Outcome
   A. Reflection

Journal Design and Purpose

As detailed below, purpose, focus, process. and outcome are the key components in the professional growth journal.

Why? (Purpose)

To participate in a professional learning community, reflect on professional practices, share observations, learnings, and suggestions as part of the evaluation process.

What If? (Focus)

Generate a banner question (the "big question") for professional inquiry.

How Will It Work? (Process)

- Make professional development plans.
- Collect artifacts and evidence.
- Participate in professional development activities.
- Establish checkpoints for the meeting.

So What? (Outcome)

- Demonstrate.
- Articulate.
- Exhibit learnings

As applied to professional development and the professional portfolio, the journaling process for educators consists of a series of actions that reflect purpose, focus, process, and outcome.

- Participate in the introduction and initial purpose-setting session.
- Establish the banner question, the focus for the portfolio.
- Identify a portfolio partner(s) and a collaboration network.
- Collect artifacts and evidence and set goals for the study.
- Plan; design a professional development plan.
- Act; engage in collaborations.
- Reflect and revise; describe outcome and evaluate the effectiveness of the journal/ portfolio process.
- Make adaptations as indicated.

Case Study: Professional Growth Journal

Following is an overview of the journaling process, demonstrating the four steps outlined above. This Case Study reflects the complete process and consists of journal pages and activities from actual professional portfolio experiences. On the journal pages in this section, participants' responses are set in italics so that the various types of reflections prompted by the journaling process can be easily identified.

When you are ready to apply the journaling process for professional growth in your own learning community, note that blanks of journal forms shown here are offered in the blacklines section (see pages 97–108). As you and your group start journaling to facilitate the professional portfolio process, you may refer to the Guide to Professional Portfolios: Types and Purpoes a useful tool on page 94 in the blacklines section.

The first step in the process is defining purpose and identifying opportunities to be explored in terms of the professional portfolio process (see Figure 3.1). This form serves as an organizer for reflections and discussions.

As with other structured journals for other frameworks for change, the journal for professional growth is organized around four steps: purpose, focus, process, and outcome. At this time, the participants orientate themselves to the entire process, but concentrate on defining purpose—reflecting on why they are doing the portfolio.

Why? (Purpose)

OBSERVATIONS • CONCERNS • QUESTIONS

- What is the purpose of the journal for professional growth/the professional portfolio?

To participate in a professional learning community, reflect on professional practices, and share observations and learnings as part of the evaluation process.

We will use the professional growth journal as a framework for initiating, planning, and facilitating our ongoing professional development, while connecting our purpose and focus for learning with the school community at-large.

The professional growth journal/professional portfolio will provide opportunities for us to

1. Focus our professional development.

2. Build and adapt a learning plan.

3. Collect artifacts and evidence.

4. Collaborate with peers, as partners and in groups.

5. Sharpen professional management skills.

6. Apply leadership abilities.

7. Draw on past experiences and knowledge.

8. Observe and contribute to collegial development.

9. Assess the impact and influence of systemic change in our school.

10. Reflect on values, attitudes, and experiences.

Figure 3.1 Sample Purpose

Learning Opportunities

Focus Development
Identify an "entry point" for professional growth. Select an area of concern, interest, and/or expertise that is a priority for you and articulate it in the form of a banner question—a leading question.

Build and Adapt a Learning Plan
Select learning activities that contribute to your learning (inquiry) process. Choose activities that can provide a variety of experiences and highlight interactions with individuals and ideas.

Collect Artifacts and Evidence
Gather data and items for portfolios that represent development and reflect new understandings in terms of professional growth.

Collaborate With Peers—as Partners and in Groups
Meet with a portfolio partner on an on-going basis and in roundtable discussion groups with other participants in the learning community. Roundtable discussions may include colleagues who have similar learning priorities, consultants, and members of the school administration/school community who are involved in the process.

Sharpen Management Skills
Identify skills that may be involved with your banner question, choosing from the standard professional skills that help you "get the job done."

Applying Leadership Abilities
Choosing from those features that are characteristic of effective leadership, identify abilities that are connected to professional growth and the portfolio process.

Draw on Past Experiences and Knowledge
Consider prior learnings and use them as a starting point for your inquiry, as you form your banner question and build a learning plan with your portfolio partner.

Observe and Contribute to Collegial Development
Create an environment in which every person is a teacher and every teacher a learner. (Throughout the journaling/portfolio process, you will have opportunities to collaborate and be both a learner and a teacher.)

Assess the Impact of Your Work on School Systems
Consider the systems within your school community that will support or interfere with the outcome of this professional portfolio process.

Reflect on Values, Attitudes, and Experiences
Meet with peers and, as a group, reflect in your journals on learning activities and classroom practices, selecting artifacts and evidence for inclusion in the process.

Figure 3.2 Sample Learning Opportunities

Defining and describing learning opportunities for the group is helpful at this time. The group participants use the Learning Opportunities form (Figure 3.2) to coach or prompt the reflective process, thereby determining the "entry point" or general theme for their portfolio work, and building a sense of learning community.

Defining a professional credo is essential to this first purpose step in the professional growth journal process. The group participants in this study use the form (see Figure 3.3) to facilitate reflection.

The next step in the professional growth journal process is establishing a focus for their professional development program, working toward a theme or "entry point." Ultimately, a banner question will be generated as a focus for learning, collaboration, and reflection as the participants use journaling to facilitate this process.

As the participants in this case start the Focus step, they reflect on the "entry point," connecting the general purpose of their work with their school system's plan for continuous improvement.

At this step of the process, the participants are mindful of the four organizers for the structured journal (Purpose, Focus, Process, and Outcome), as they concentrate on their focus for learning. Participants often use this as an opportunity to reflect with a portfolio partner, seeking to identify a focus for their particular professional portfolio plans. At this point, the group establishes a schedule for "checkpoints" (group meetings) for future conversations and collaborations that are integral to the journaling process.

Defining Your Professional Credo

I.   What are your beliefs about the purpose of your profession?

I believe that it is my job to provide students with the skills necessary for both success in their chosen careers and lives—in general. I feel it is my job to expose them to a wide variety of subjects and experiences, in order to give them the opportunity to explore their interests and talents.

II. Describe the ideal curriculum.

A curriculum in which several disciplines are connected and address a variety of learning styles or intelligences.

A curriculum that provides students with as many chances as possible to express themselves in a creative manner, and to experience success.

A curriculum that offers students useful, relevant skills.

III. What are your beliefs about how students learn?

I believe that students learn by using a combination of their intelligences. I especially feel that they learn best when they are allowed choices in how they express facts and concepts studied in the classroom. In addition, I believe the content presented must be meaningful and relevant to the students.

Figure 3.3 Sample Professional Credo

To facilitate the Focus step, the group uses a graphic organizer such as a Venn diagram (see Figure 3.4) to organize reflections and "coaching collaborations" with portfolio partners. Each participant takes five to seven minutes to generate a list of actions that he or she *needs* to do, and a list of those actions he or she wishes or *wants* to do. The *need-to-dos* are actions that are required in professional teaching practice in their particular classrooms. The *want-to-dos* are innovative or new actions individual members have an interest in doing—actions that, from their perspectives, would enhance their work.

After the lists have been generated, each participant takes five minutes to share his or her needs and wants with a partner, each taking a turn being a listener. The listener's role is to listen well enough to later pose thoughtful questions that will assist the partner in identifying an emerging theme. Each participant endeavors to listen and ask questions of the partner, coaching that person in focusing on and identifying the theme, *not* telling that person what he or she thinks the theme is.

The following tools in the blacklines section will prove useful in this collaborative listening process so important to the focus step of the professional growth journaling process: Guide for Listening (page 80); Directions for Coaching Triads (page 77); Banner Questions Guide (page 71); and Professional Development Checklist (page 73).

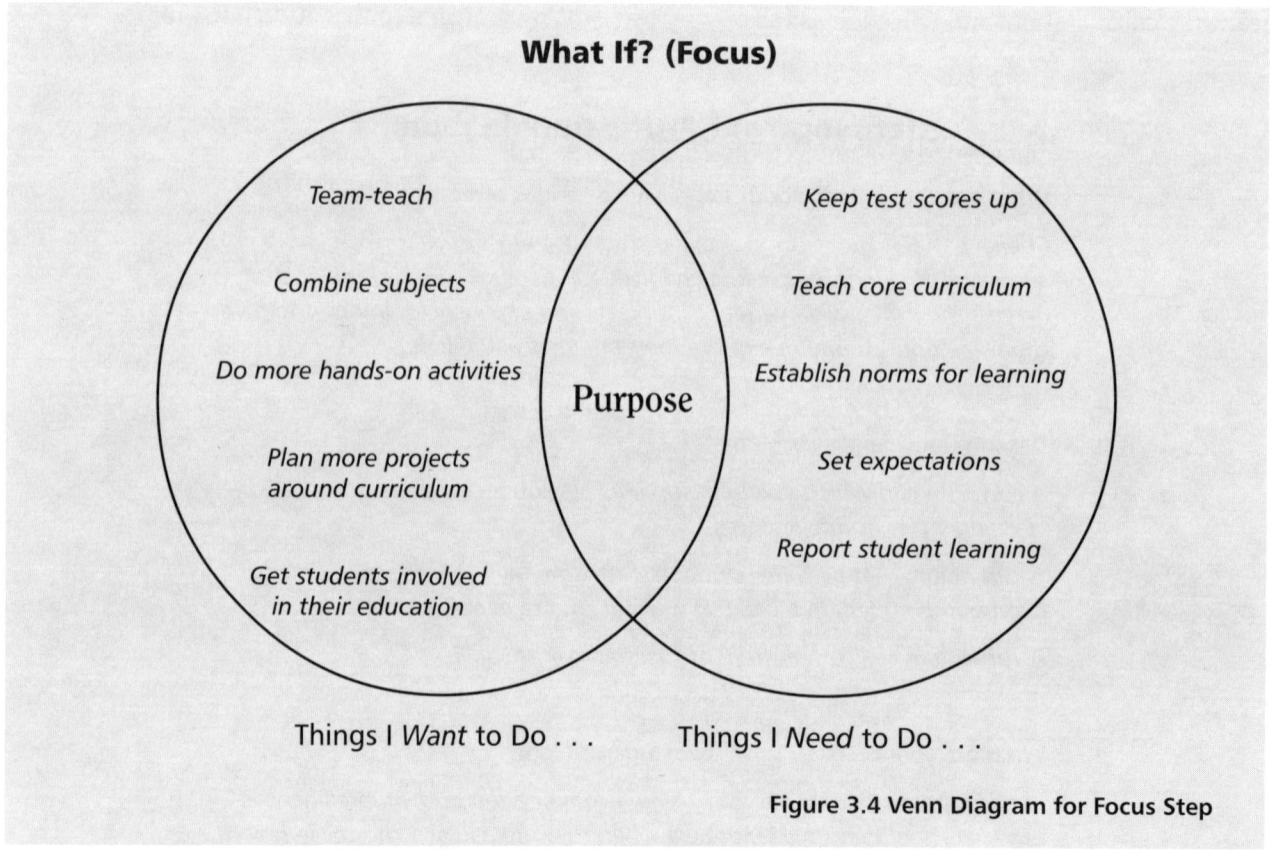

What If? (Focus)

Team-teach

Combine subjects

Do more hands-on activities

Plan more projects around curriculum

Get students involved in their education

Purpose

Keep test scores up

Teach core curriculum

Establish norms for learning

Set expectations

Report student learning

Things I *Want* to Do . . .   Things I *Need* to Do . . .

Figure 3.4 Venn Diagram for Focus Step

After participants have identified their general goals in professional development, they use the Banner Question form (see Figure 3.5) to formulate the essential question that will guide their individual plans for professional development. Again, the participants may refer to the Banner Questions Guide, the tool on page 71 of the blackline masters section, to facilitate this process.

Establishing a banner question (the "big idea") during the journaling process is not an easy task, no matter what framework for change is being used, whether it be action research, the professional portfolio, staff development, the school portfolio, or the study group. A New York City teacher-center facilitator once commented, "Banner questions are not written in stone—more like gelatin." Banner questions re-form, change shape, and are flexible. Formulating *splinter questions,* which are smaller questions that constitute subsets of the proposed banner question, helps guide and clarify the focusing process.

During this process, participants find it helpful to offer sample questions and share possible new questions. This strategy spurs thinking among members, encouraging each participant to formulate a banner question before proceeding to the Process step of the professional growth journaling process.

Banner Question

How do we create interdisciplinary instruction in our middle school?

Splinter Questions

What are the benefits of interdisciplinary instruction?

How do we group students at present?

How can we pull in other disciplines (such as math in with social studies)?

How can we facilitate student reflection?

How can we find a balance between process and content?

How should we infuse competencies such as SCANs?

How can we address relevance of content to students?

How should we involve students in the assessment and learning process?

Figure 3.5 Sample Banner Question

When the group meets at this point, the individuals review their banner questions. Often these questions have changed from the last meeting—that is what continuous learning is all about! During a group meeting at this point, they use the following How Will It Work? (Process) form (see Figure 3.6), as they begin to design a professional development plan.

At this time, the participants review the "checkpoint" dates (two or three meeting times scheduled in the future), which are important times for collaboration and sharing progress. To facilitate such meetings, the group uses the Professional Development Checklist on page 73 in the blacklines section.

How Will It Work? (Process)

PLAN • DATA COLLECTION • COLLABORATION

- Make professional growth and development plans.
- Collect artifacts and evidence as part of the portfolio process.
- Participate in professional development activities.
- Establish points to cover for next meeting.

Professional Development Plan

Focusing on the development of a plan, you establish collaborations to facilitate and support learning. Your professional development activities should be selected in terms of your individual classroom teaching situations and the context of your banner questions.

The plan will contain your

1. Credo

2. Banner question

3. Professional development activities

4. Outcome, as well as any "re-thinkings" and applications to professional/ classroom practices

The professional development plan will facilitate perusal and integrate learning from the inquiry. Begin with activities you are currently involved in. Continue to add activities to your plan as you move through the portfolio process and collaborate with others. Some examples of professional development activities are

- Visiting other schools

- Attending seminars

- Observing teaching and group facilitation activities in progress

- Meeting with other educators who share your interests

- Inviting a colleague to observe you at a meeting or professional workshop

- Reading articles from professional journals

- Joining a study group in the school community

- Researching a theme or concept related to your banner question

Figure 3.6 Sample Process

An important journaling activity for the professional growth/portfolio process is the maintenance of a professional development log. The group participants in this study use the Professional Development Log form (see Figure 3.7) to facilitate this step, ultimately setting a schedule for professional growth and development—the portfolio process.

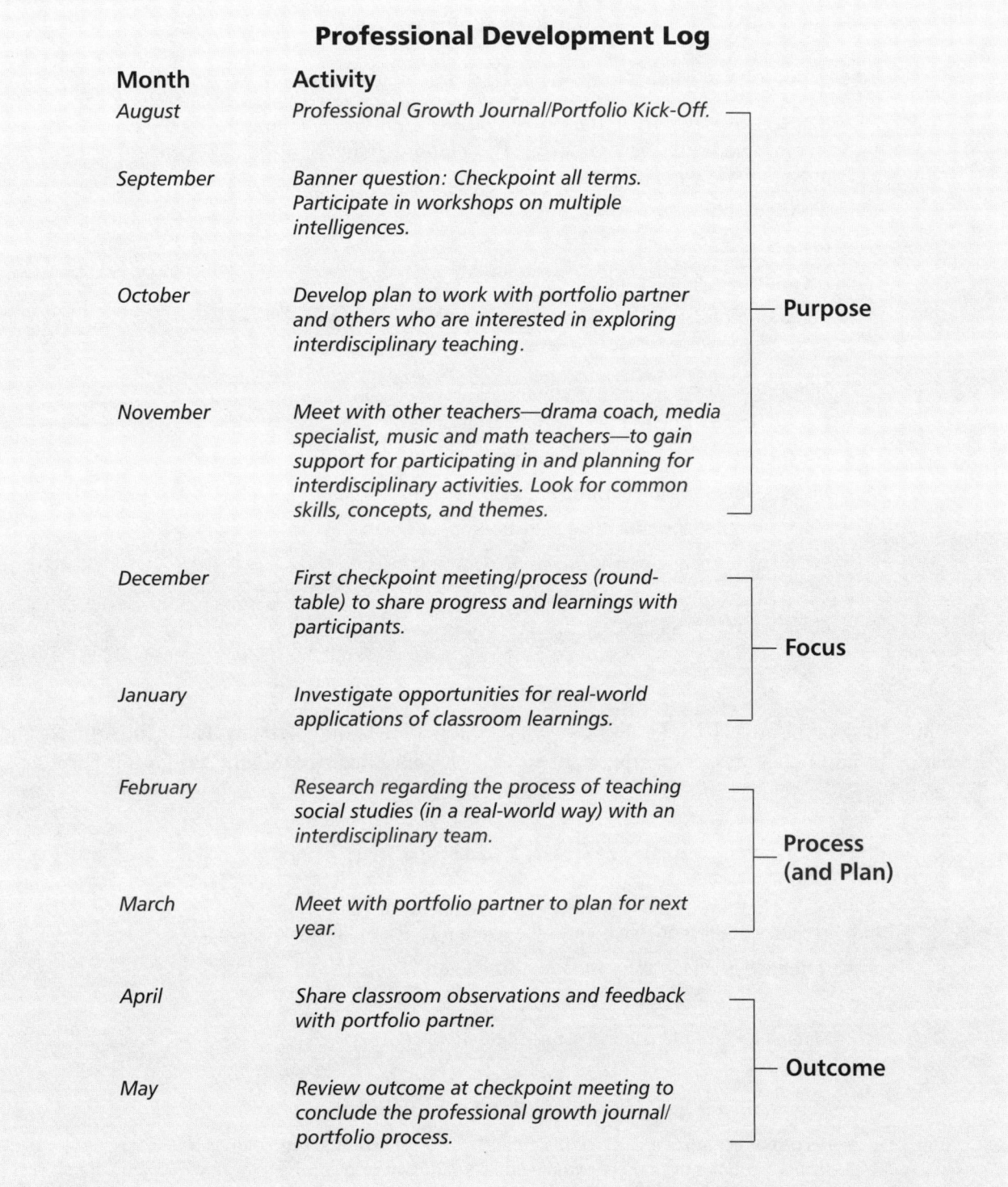

Professional Development Log

Month	Activity	
August	Professional Growth Journal/Portfolio Kick-Off.	
September	Banner question: Checkpoint all terms. Participate in workshops on multiple intelligences.	
October	Develop plan to work with portfolio partner and others who are interested in exploring interdisciplinary teaching.	**Purpose**
November	Meet with other teachers—drama coach, media specialist, music and math teachers—to gain support for participating in and planning for interdisciplinary activities. Look for common skills, concepts, and themes.	
December	First checkpoint meeting/process (round-table) to share progress and learnings with participants.	**Focus**
January	Investigate opportunities for real-world applications of classroom learnings.	
February	Research regarding the process of teaching social studies (in a real-world way) with an interdisciplinary team.	**Process (and Plan)**
March	Meet with portfolio partner to plan for next year.	
April	Share classroom observations and feedback with portfolio partner.	**Outcome**
May	Review outcome at checkpoint meeting to conclude the professional growth journal/portfolio process.	

Figure 3.7 Sample Professional Development Log

A facilitator during this phase of the journaling process uses the Guide to Reflection on Professional Growth (on page 75 of the blacklines section) to prompt rethinking.

Next, the group moves to intensive collaboration with colleagues as part of the Process step, using the Collaborations journal form (Figure 3.8) to reflect on the progress made.

Collaborations

When you meet with your colleagues during this stage of the professional growth journaling/portfolio process, reflect on your daily decisions and other experiences related to your inquiry. Discuss the integration and connections among the standards for your profession and if you are "aligned on purpose"—that is, if you have defined a common purpose for your work.

To facilitate collaboration. . .

- Discuss issues.
- Focus on banner question.
- Consider professional development activities.
- Discuss recent experiences.
- Share your professional development plan.
- Plan to observe and/or meet with a partner.
- Ask for feedback or input regarding a decision.
- Make adaptations to your professional development plan.
- Ask for suggestions regarding activities for your plan.
- Exhibit artifacts and/or evidence from your portfolio.
- Share current findings or learnings.

Figure 3.8 Sample Collaborations Form

Keeping track of the artifacts and evidence collected in the portfolio process is an important function. Group participants use the Artifacts and Evidence Registry (Figure 3.9) for this purpose.

Artifacts and Evidence Registry

Briefly list below any artifacts and evidence, gathered for your professional portfolio, that prompt reflection or collaboration in relation to your banner question.

- *Notebook of lesson plans for social studies and English.*
- *Newspapers/news articles.*
- *Materials related to content scope and sequence.*
- *Examples of student projects/student work.*
- *Notes from principal, portfolio partner, and/or students.*
- *Record of activities and accomplishments by after-school clubs such as the student council or homecoming celebration committee.*

Figure 3.9 Sample Artifacts and Evidence Registry

The fourth step of the journaling process is articulating Outcome. Participants in the group use the So What? (Outcome) journal form (see Figure 3.10) to prompt thoughtful reflection.

So What? (Outcome)

DEMONSTRATE • ARTICULATE • EXHIBIT LEARNINGS

Reflections, Rethinking, Conclusions, and Learnings

As I reflect back on the year, I have learned a great deal from working with my portfolio partner and teaching team. My banner question has focused me and I have gained new understandings about my work, leading me to many conversations with colleagues. At times I was unsure of the outcome and benefits—now I see so many possibilities.

The portfolio process helped to focus our collaborations. I got to know other staff members who participated in the portfolio process, and now better understand and appreciate their work.

I have come to realize the extreme effort it takes to build an interdisciplinary team and to address our many different needs, attitudes, content areas, and teaching practices. That is, in fact, what makes the work with interdisciplinary studies such a rich experience for students and teachers!

I have learned a lot from working with my banner question this year, but I am not ready to abandon it yet. I feel I have just begun and hope to take this question to another level next year. I am excited about the positive results we have seen in student learning and involvement.

What articulation, sharing, demonstrating, and exhibiting have you done in regard to your professional portfolio?

My team members and I have shared one of our interdisciplinary units with the rest of the school staff. We hope to gain more support and interest in expanding this idea with our fellow educators.

What new questions have emerged from your inquiry and development?

I would like to continue with my current banner question and take it further. A splinter question is, How can we gain schoolwide support to look at interdisciplinary instruction in the middle school setting? An additional question I have is, Why is there is such resistance to try new ways?

How have your beliefs or practices been challenged or changed?

I have been challenged by trying to find the time to meet and plan with team members. I know we are always pressed for time, but this kind of planning is very time-consuming. Possibly it will take less time after we have become more experienced with the process.

A possible future banner question?

I want to stay with the same banner question for next term. My portfolio partner and I are looking forward to going deeper into the planning and design of interdisciplinary teaching.

Figure 3.10 Sample Outcome

Professional Growth Wrap-Up

Engaging in the professional growth journal/ portfolio process provides you with a framework for reflection on teaching practices and collaboration with colleagues. Isolation is a significant job hazard for the teaching profession, while sharing concerns, successes, and visiting other classes and schools opens new vistas for professional growth. Using journaling as a process in terms of your professional portfolio provides a way to focus on a particular interest or concern related to your work. Opportunities for reflection and collaborations with others in your professional community are the key benefits.

The professional growth journal process, based on the following four steps, serves as a guide to "coach" you and the learning community of which you are a part. Walking through the process once more, you

- Start with a *purpose*. (Why are you doing this portfolio?)

- Identify a *focus*. (What questions are you asking about your work?)

- Design a plan or *process;* collect artifacts; and collaborate. (How will you engage in professional activities?)

- Reflect on an *outcome*. (What have you learned and how will you attach your learnings to your work in the classroom?)

Helpful Hints

Be patient with identifying your banner question during the Focus step of the journaling process. Establishing a banner question does take time. Do not be surprised if you change it several times. During the professional growth journal/portfolio process, it is not uncommon for individuals (or the learning community as a whole) to discover that they have uncovered a piece of work that is bigger than anticipated. Use the splinter questions technique to focus and modify your inquiry along the way. These smaller questions break off of the BIG question and aim you in a direction that will impact your professional growth and development.

Reflection and Conversation

Identifying Opportunities for Using the Professional Growth Journal

1. How might this journaling process enhance a continuing education/graduate studies program?

2. My professional portfolio could be incorporated into an alternative teacher assessment process by . . .

3. How might I use this journaling/portfolio process to help select professional workshops to attend?

4. Whom might I invite to be my portfolio partner?

5. We could start a roundtable discussion among several portfolio partners in our learning community by bringing up . . .

6. How will we include our school/site administrator in the process?

Chapter 4

Staff Development Journal

"It is not enough to target staff development as a top priority for reform efforts. Leaders who are serious about educational reforms must take into account the nature of teachers as adult learners." (Moye 1997, 7)

Background of Staff Development

Traditionally, staff development within school districts has consisted of one-day inservice workshops on new educational theories, and new methodologies or changes that have been mandated for the school community. Often those participating in and managing such workshops have expressed concern about the effeciveness of such staff development, questioning its worth and whether there is transfer of learning to actual classroom practices. In recent years, educators have questioned what effective staff development is and how they can determine its impact on student learning. It is important to note that over the years the purpose, meaning, function, and design of professional development—in general—have changed. Viewing staff development as it is today—a framework for change, educators will find that the process addresses them as adult

learners and supports the implementation and integration of new ideas into classroom practices.

How to Use the Staff Development Journal

The traditional approach to helping educators learn has been to develop the skills of individuals to do their work. Staff development needs to enhance the collective capacity of people to create and pursue overall visions (Senge 1995, 9).

Using a structured journal to guide the staff development process can impact the long-range goal of professional development. Journaling is an effective tool for reflection, allowing teachers to use the staff development process effectively and to assess the impact of new teaching practices in the classroom.

Ideally, the decisions and designs in effective staff development plans are rooted in learner-centered theories and philosophical beliefs. The following principles, reflecting a teacher-as-learner approach, serve as guidelines to create effective staff development environments:

- Invite learners (professional educators) to use their creative abilities, talents, interests, and concerns as mediums to reach a deeper level of learning, involvement, and professional commitment.

- Use inquiry as a foundational tool to engage the learners, encouraging them to seek answers to their own questions as well as those posed by their colleagues.

- Facilitate the process by identifying the learners' current perceptions and levels of understanding in the context of a particular development plan, concept, theory, or concern. Use this data to make informed decisions about adapting and customizing the process.

- Allow opportunities for feedback, reflective writing, and collaborations in an effort to internalize conceptual understandings and build learning communities.

- Encourage learners to identify their entry points (strongest modes of learning) for planning and demonstrating the integration of new ideas into their classroom practices.

These principles for adult learning coupled with knowledge about the process of school improvement lead to staff development as a framework for change, one that provides opportunities for truly effective professional development.

In writing about staff development, Thomas Guskey (1994) offered the following attributes as considerations for "results-oriented" professional development:

1. Recognize that change is both an individual and an organizational process.

2. Think big but start small.

3. Work in teams to maintain support.

4. Include procedures for feedback on results.

5. Provide continued follow-up support and pressure for continuous improvement.

In an article on professional and staff development, Linda Darling-Hammond (1996) addresses criticism of teachers today, pointing out that it is not a question of teachers not doing their jobs. The fact is the that their jobs have changed. As in other professions, the new practices professional educators are being asked to employ require building capacity and working collaboratively for continuous improvement. It is important that teachers be supported in the learning process through effective staff development.

The process of journaling allows teachers to reflect on the learning process, assessing the impact of their professional development activities on classroom practices and student learning.

Organization

The structured journal process for staff development, as for the other frameworks for change, is built around four steps: Purpose, Focus, Process, and Outcome. Each learner (professional educator) keeps his or her own journal or portfolio for the development session(s).

Journal Design and Process

The purpose of the journal is to provide a framework for organizing, constructing, implementing, and reflecting on the particular staff development plan. Following is a template for using the staff development journal, denoting the actions that characterize the four steps in the process.

Why? (Purpose)

- Establish the reason for the particular staff development plan and how it connects to the schoolwide focus; orientate yourself with staff development as a framework for change.

What If? (Focus)

- Identify the theme or domain for professional learning. Describe how you anticipate learnings from participation in staff development sessions will enhance student learning and the quality of your professional work.

How Will It Work? (Process)

- Consider activities and adaptations you might try by way of implementing learnings from the staff development sessions into classroom practices.

- As you work through the plan, practice sample learning activities and reflect on the outcomes. Test your design.

- Ask, How are these strategies working with students?

So What? (Outcome)

- Conclude participation in the staff development experience with final reflections. Share reflections with your colleagues as you demonstrate and describe learnings that have taken place.

The primary purpose of staff development is to allow professionals, working in learning communities, to reflect on professional practices and connect new learnings to current practices. The staff development journal will focus and organize that process. The expectation is that participants will use the journal process, along with content knowledge, to work effectively toward change.

Case Study: Staff Development Journal

"This final reform—weaving continuous learning into the fabric of the teaching job—will be the one that makes the difference if we can act in a concerted fashion in every school and community to take the teaching job as it is now defined and confined and extend it into a true profession" (Renyi 1996, 30).

Following is an overview of the journaling process, including samples of journals and activities from actual staff development experiences. On the journal pages in this section, participants' responses are set in italics so that the various types of reflections that are prompted by the journaling process can be easily identified.

When you, as a facilitator or learning community member, are ready to apply the journaling process in your own staff development sessions, note that blanks of the staff development journal forms shown here are offered in the blacklines section (see pages 109–112).

The journal pages can be presented and used in a variety of ways, depending on the needs of the participants. All the journal pages may be introduced at the first session, to orientate the participants to the entire process; or the journal pages may be gradually introduced in a series of staff development sessions. If time allows, each development session may focus on one journal page at a time.

The questions in the Why? (Purpose) form (see Figure 4.1) regard the nature and goal of staff development in general, prompting each participant to reflect on his or her role as a teacher, on personal goals for the staff development in this particular case, and on the individuals's theory of learning.

Why? (Purpose)

1. Describe the role of teacher as facilitator of student learning.

   I think the teacher is a facilitator because he or she must listen to and observe the child. Therefore, the teacher is mediating or modifying curriculum to meet the needs of the child. This process is a two-way communication process. I consider that communication to be facilitation, rather than the perception some have about teaching as a one-way telling process.

2. What do you see as the primary purpose of the staff development?

   I am participating in the sessions to learn more about differentiated curriculum. Teachers from my school attended last year and have shared the instructional units they developed. I would like to do the same with my class.

3. What are your personal theories about how children learn?

   I think children learn all the time. How they learn in school is another issue. They probably learn in school when they are interested and feel successful. This could require a variety of methods and modalities. The challenge is these methods should vary from child to child, which creates an even greater challenge when you have a large and diverse class.

Figure 4.1 Sample Purpose

The participants move on to the Focus step with a review of the four parts of the journal (Purpose, Focus, Process, and Outcome). Using the What If? (Focus) form (see Figure 4.2), the participants zero in on the application area for learnings from the staff development plan.

During this step of the process, the individuals focus on and clarify the purpose of the staff development—in this case, a particular instructional area. In other cases, the focus may be on a new teaching standard or theme in student learning. At this point, site administrators and members from other leadership groups in the school community are invited to participate. They facilitate the sharing of information, responding to teachers' questions regarding the school community's long-term planning and desired outcomes or expectations. A staff developer (or sponsor for the development session) is present to support the learning/journaling process.

Moving to the third step of journaling, the participants use the How Will It Work? (Process) journal form (see Figure 4.3). The participants decide to use this form as a "checkpoint" tool at each staff development session, so they can reflect and provide regular feedback to the facilitator on their learnings. They also address the need to make adaptations when a new program is due to be implemented. (See the List of Facilitation Strategies on page 78 in the blacklines section, a useful tool to facilitate this process.)

What If? (Focus)

1. The instructional area I have chosen in which to apply learnings from this staff development is . . .

   An interdisciplinary unit for my language arts program. This year we will be reading different fairy tales. I thought it might be interesting to develop a variety of learning center activities, designed for different levels of participation, possibly using a multiple intelligences design for the activities.

2. The staff development will alter my current practices, since . . .

   Currently I have not been very successful with the learning centers in my class. My students do not seem to be working independently in an effective manner. The activities I would like to work on in this staff development could improve the effectiveness of the centers, giving me more individual time for student conferences.

Figure 4.2 Sample Focus

How Will It Work? (Process)

Date: *April 9*

Session: *Multiple Intelligences (MI) at Work*

I expected to learn . . .

about MI and how I might apply it in my classes.

I learned . . .

about "entry points"—for instance, how to use MI as an entry point of my students' individual learning needs.

I plan to . . .

share examples with my students and see if they can identify a preferred intelligence for their learning.

Next time I . . .

need more practical examples.

Figure 4.3 Sample Process

During the final step (Outcome), the staff developer and others members of the school community who have sponsored the staff development sessions are present to review participants' responses and reflections on the entire experience. This final session with the participants has been arranged ahead of time and, with the permission of all involved, copies of the completed So What? (Outcome) journal forms (see Figure 4.4) are made available—in order to be reviewed by the learning community as a whole. The teachers, facilitators, and other participants look for patterns of learnings in the various responses, discussing the impact the sessions have had on classroom practices and implications for the school system's long-term planning.

So What? (Outcome)

CONCLUSIONS, REFLECTIONS, ADAPTATIONS, MODIFICATIONS, LEARNINGS

- What articulating, sharing, demonstrating and exhibiting have you done with your peers in regarding to your learnings?

  Several colleagues have visited my class to observe my students in action with the new strategies I have learned in our staff development sessions.

- What new questions about your study and strategies have emerged from participation in the staff development?

  I now see a need for learning center activities to be at the students' independent levels.

- How have your beliefs about student needs changed?

  I am much more aware of individual needs and the importance of meeting those needs.

- Future plans for using the new practices should include . . .

  Opportunities to observe and collaborate with fellow teachers.

Figure 4.4 Sample Outcome

Staff Development Wrap-Up

There has been a growing interest in assessing the impact of staff development, often used interchangeably with professional development, on student learning. Professional development has evolved from workshops that "teach" curriculum and programs to learning communities that are committed to student learning outcomes. In light of this commitment, professional educators are now seen as teacher-learners.

The staff development journal provides you with the structure and process for reflecting on your professional work and connecting learnings from staff development to your classroom. The learnings from the journal process can also serve as data or evidence of teacher learnings, so that the quality of the staff development and the connection to working with students may be assessed.

Using the structured journal as a guide, you

- Identify a *purpose* for participation in staff development.

- *Focus* on a theme or teaching standard.

- Design a *plan* and *process* for applying learnings to classroom practices.

- Consider the *outcome* of the staff development and collect evidence of the impact of your work on student learning.

Helpful Hints

Use the staff development journal to connect learnings to classroom practices and to give feedback to professional workshop instructors or sponsors. The journal can assist in making decisions regarding the design and ongoing support of future staff development offerings.

Reflection and Conversation

Identifying Opportunities for Staff Development

1. I can use my journal to assess the quality of the staff development program I am participating in by . . .

2. How does the content and process of the staff development experience connect with my work with students?

3. What have I learned about myself as a learner that is similar to my experiences with students? What is different?

4. How can I connect action research to staff development to assess the impact of new practices on student learning?

5. This journal may influence the decision process for future staff development in my school community by . . .

6. How can we build commitment to quality staff development in my school community?

Chapter 5

School Portfolio Journal

"Community building must become the heart of any school improvement effort . . . it requires us to think community, believe in community, and practice community." (Sergiovanni 1994, xi)

Background of the School Portfolio

The school portfolio as a framework for change can be used for a variety of purposes. It is often used as a communication method to report on the status of school programs and student progress to the community at large, as well a way to celebrate accomplishments and plan for the future. A flexible tool, the portfolio can be used as part of the process schools go through as they apply for educational grants.

As presented in this chapter, the school portfolio, facilitated through the journaling process, provides a framework for learning community members to demonstrate accomplishments and establish priorities for the school or school district. Such a portfolio may feature a rubric or guide to assess where the school community is in the change process, identifying strengths as well as weaknesses.

How to Use the School Portfolio Journal

The school portfolio journal is a process designed to facilitate the school community as they articulate, demonstrate, and illustrate their purpose, programs, and progress. Like the other frameworks presented in this book, the school portfolio is organized around four steps (Purpose, Focus, Process, and Outcome). As envisioned in the Case Study in this chapter, those involved in the school portfolio process often devote a session or meeting to each step. Activities at each phase guide the participants in focusing and directing their efforts. After collecting artifacts and evidence to demonstrate learnings and establishing plans for school programs and classroom practices, participants share their observations, reflections, and priorities as part of the process. The portfolio process, facilitated by journaling, culminates in a final product, the school portfolio.

Journal Organization, Design, and Process

The first step of the journaling process is to clarify the Purpose for the portfolio. Is it for planning for school improvement, facilitating the change process, organizing for an educational grant application, or telling the story of the school's journey and accomplishments for the year?

The second step (Focus) is to define the programs and/or priorities that school community members have identified as the subject for the portfolio. This process allows the learning community involved in the school portfolio (which often includes teachers, parents, administrators, community leaders, local business people, and consultants) to work together in identifying all the parts of the total program. If the journaling process is being used to demonstrate school community accomplishments, the portfolio group might focus on those aspects of the school program that contributed to those successes. On the other hand, if the process is being used to assess the current status of the school and to develop a plan for change, the group may identify priorities by using a graphic organizer—such as the Action Priorities Wheel presented in this chapter's Case Study.

The Process step leads the group to the constructing of the school portfolio. If multiple priorities or programs have been identified, participants can break themselves down into small groups and devote themselves to a particular priority or program. Using journaling to facilitate the process, the small group members may ask what the purpose of the program or priority is; what specific area of schooling it focuses on; how the process will work as well as how the program or priority will be integrated with the whole school portfolio; and what will the outcome (the accomplishments) will be. When each small group has gone through this process, all the participants can reconvene in a "portfolio working session," at which time learnings and plans for the portfolio can be shared with the whole learning community.

The Outcome step is designed as a way to review the school portfolio journaling process and final product, as well as to determine future goals and actions for the school community in general.

Case Study: School Portfolio Journal

Following is an overview of the journaling process, including samples of journals and activities from actual school portfolio experiences. On the journal pages in this section, participants' responses are set in italics so that the various types of notes and reflections that are prompted by the journaling process can be easily identified. Commentary is provided before each form, explaining how the group under study applied the journaling process to the school portfolio.

When you, as a facilitator or learning community member, are ready to apply the journaling process with your colleagues, note that blanks of the journal forms for the school portfolio shown here are offered in the blacklines section (see pages 113–121).

To begin the school portfolio process, the group in this Case Study designs a cover for their portfolio—much like a masthead of a publication (see Figure 5.1).

In the school portfolio process, all members of the community should have an opportunity to participate, as they wish. The facilitators in this particular case study have invited parents, teachers, and administrators, as well as other school staff and local business people who are in partnership with the school, to join in the process of articulating priorities and accomplishments.

Agreement regarding purpose, or defining their shared purpose and desired outcome, is a critical starting point. It builds the foundation for effective design and process of the portfolio. The portfolio can best serve as a connection between the institution and the individual when a joint purpose is clearly agreed upon from the start.

Portfolio

School Name

Monroe Avenue Elementary School

School Portfolio Team

Helen Campbell, Principal

Names of team members

_____

_____

_____

_____

_____

_____

_____

Figure 5.1 Sample School Portfolio Cover

Using the Guide for Defining Purpose (see Figure 5.2) to coach the process, the group begins to determine the purpose of the school portfolio.

Guide for Defining Purpose

The school portfolio is an organizer for planning and reflecting on continuous school improvement. It is a framework for working together to identify school priorities and exhibit student learning outcomes.

The school portfolio process provides a structure for

- Facilitating change.
- Working together as a staff and school community.
- Organizing, planning, and assessing student outcomes.
- Collecting artifacts and evidences.
- Building community relationships.
- Reflecting on values and attitudes.
- Drawing on past experiences and knowledge.
- Exploring possibilities.
- Building new understandings about priorities.

(continued on next page)

To work toward defining a purpose, the school portfolio team members will

1. Consider their definition of common purpose and formulate and share their philosophy, highlighting belief systems about the purpose and process of education.

2. Learn about the portfolio process as a tool for organizing school planning.

3. Build communication abilities and listening skills.

Figure 5.2 Guide for Defining Purpose

Next, the team members move toward consensus in the Purpose step as they go through the journaling process. The portfolio team has

- Clarified the context for decision making with school administration.

- Determined a standard or rubric for their work.

- Set parameters for their collaboration.

At this point, team members go to the Why? (Purpose) journal form (see Figure 5.3), reflecting personally on the role of schooling in their community as part of the school portfolio process. (A facilitator may also use the following tools in the blacklines section: Worksheet for Defining Purpose and Priorities, page 82; School Portfolio Survey, page 83; and Strategy for Determining Top Priorities for School Change, page 84.)

Why? (Purpose)

1. From my perspective the primary indicators of student learning are . . .

When students are asking questions, engaged with a high level of energy in their school work, and making steady progress academically. Their actual written work is a product, but not always the only or best indicator that they are—in fact—learning. I think we need to observe our students and ask them questions in order to be assured learning is taking place.

2. My personal theory about how students learn is . . .

Kids learn from doing and from having someone be with them and guide them as they practice new skills. They learn when they are in a risk-free environment in which they are not afraid to try and try again. All kids do not learn the same way: Some learn by talking and others by doing. Others learn by watching and listening. We need to accommodate a variety of learning styles and student needs.

3. At our school I am most proud of . . .

The way we all work together as a school community. Even though we do not always agree on an issue, we are willing to talk about it. An outstanding accomplishment is our student-run school store, which provides products that display school spirit and teaches students real-world business skills.

Figure 5.3 Sample Purpose

Moving on to the Focus step, the school portfolio team uses the journaling process to focus their work, establishing priorities, or entry points, to demonstrate and exhibit current achievements within the school portfolio frame-work. Using the What If? (Focus) form (see Figure 5.4) to coach the process, they discuss and reflect on needs and goals for continuous school improvement.

What If? (Focus)

At the Focus phase of the process, the school portfolio team will

1. Define the priorities for the school community.

2. Select the top six or eight priorities using the Action Priority Wheel (Figure 5.5).

3. Form priority work groups accordingly.

Ideally, each priority work group is a mixture of parents, teachers, and other school community members. The teachers can check in with colleagues regarding the collections of artifacts and program descriptions. The parents and other members can enhance the process with their various perspectives. The process of conversations and collaborations within these groups builds school community.

Figure 5.4 Sample Focus

During the Focus step of the school portfolio process, the team members collaborate and design structures to work together in priority action teams. The team uses the Action Priority Wheel exercise (see Figure 5.5) to facilitate this process, as they engage in the following steps:

1. Brainstorm all ideas, suggestions, needs, and wants.

2. Break into small groups and combine similar ideas, forming a list of priorities within these small groups.

3. Reconvene and share the small-group priority lists; compile a master priority list that represents priorities for all participating community members.

4. Post the priority list at the front of the room.

5. Cast votes for priorities by using peel-and-stick colored dots—or by making slash marks with a marker pen—on the chart paper next to their priority(s) of choice. (Each team member is allowed three votes. The team members are aware they may use all three votes for one priority or divide their votes in any manner they wish.)

6. Place the top six or eight priorities in the Action Wheel. The wheel image illustrates or implies that all priorities are important and interdependent. (A member may select "explore student outcomes" as her priority, yet she is well aware that all aspects of the learning process contribute to student outcomes.)

7. Work in the priority action groups of choice, based on the voting process. Members use the prompts on the Action Wheel to guide their group sessions as they clarify the current and future efforts in their priority area, discussing how they will represent purpose and progress.

Addressing what artifacts to include in the school portfolio that will represent their accomplishments and commitment, the members reflect on how they are currently supporting and achieving their priority. Group members include a discussion of future plans in their priority area.

Action Priority Wheel

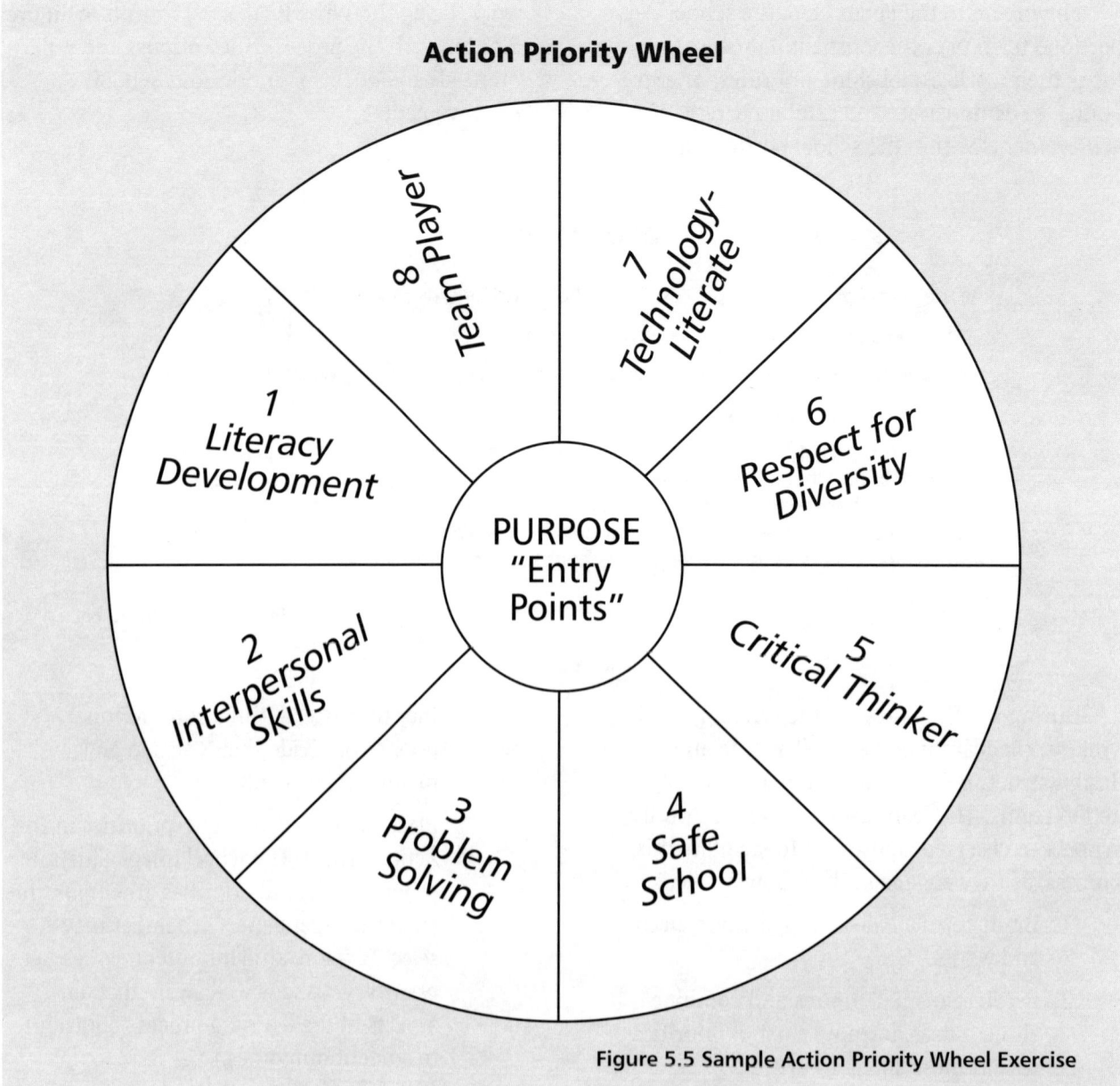

Figure 5.5 Sample Action Priority Wheel Exercise

At this point, the school portfolio team in this Case Study have several types of three-ring binders or containers handy, so they are prepared to organize and display the various artifacts (evidence such as a student achievement chart) that will tell the "story" about the priorities and accomplishments of the school. As the team members enter this phase of the process, they are prepared to use the same presentation format to introduce their priorities and to describe current and future efforts. The various groups exhibit their artifacts and evidence to illustrate their desired outcomes. Ideally, when these individual priority groups combine their work, the end product (the school portfolio) has continuity in terms of design.

Using the How Will It Work? (Process) form (see Figure 5.6) as a facilitation tool, the team moves on to the third step of the school portfolio process. A facilitator uses the Student Profile Checklist (see page 76 in the blacklines section) to identify student outcomes as part of the collaboration, process, determining a shared purpose and priorities for the school portfolio.

How Will It Work? (Process)

At the process phase, the team will

1. Agree on a design and format for the school portfolio.
2. Meet with community members in their individual priority action teams.
3. Identify existing and future programs and practices that contribute to the various priorities.
4. Consider future programs and practices to support priorities for change.
5. Describe impact of existing programs.
6. Collect artifacts and evidences of accomplishments.
7. Agree on a plan for checkpoints (meetings to ascertain progress), as well as a time line for completion of the school portfolio.

Figure 5.6 Sample Process

Each priority action team uses the Priority Action Team Worksheet (see Figure 5.7) to prompt reflection on the focus of their work together. For purposes of this Case Study, one priority action team has chosen "literacy development" as the priority on which to focus.

Priority Action Team Worksheet

Priority Description
Our school priority is literacy development. We feel literacy (listening, speaking, reading, and writing) is the key to school success and learning.

Current Accomplishments:
We have literacy portfolios, collections of various students' writings and reflections (journalings) about favorite stories they have read. The portfolios also contain a book actually written and bound by the students.

We have published authors visit our school two times a year to speak with the students about becoming a writer and the importance of dedication to writing as well as reading books.

We have established a Parents-and-Reading Club that meets with the reading specialist once a month. At these meetings, parents learn about the reading and writing process, how their students are being instructed, and how they can support the learning process at home. There is always time for discussing special interests and concerns expressed by parents, which often assists in planning a topic for the next session.

Literacy portfolio sharing: Students visit other classrooms every Friday to share individual portfolios with a partner. Each partner writes notes in the visitor's portfolio registry, commenting on the portfolio, recording the event with the date, and signing his or her name.

Future Plans and Suggestions:
In the future, we plan to have Family Library Night when family members accompany students for an evening at the school library, expressly for selecting and reading books together. We are also in the process of designing a process for individualized literacy plans for each student. These plans will be customized to meet students' various developing needs in each area of the reading process.

Senior citizens will be visiting our classes to read to students and to contribute to their reading logs on a regular basis.

Figure 5.7 Sample Priority Action Team Worksheet

SkyLight Training and Publishing Inc.

At this point, priority team members consult with others for information and bring program descriptions from their various classrooms or school sites, as well as seek ideas for future plans to bring to the next scheduled checkpoint meeting. At checkpoint meetings during the Focus step, the small group members

- Share programs and descriptions.
- Use a journaling form that will "fit in" with the agreed-upon school portfolio format.
- Share artifacts and select the most appropriate ones for programs and special event descriptions.

- Write descriptions of artifacts for the school portfolio.
- Reaffirm next checkpoint meeting date, making sure the priority team is on schedule with the agreed-upon time line for the school portfolio team as a whole.

Each priority action group completes the Artifacts and Evidence Registry (see Figure 5.8) to facilitate the record-keeping that is essential for this step of the process. Eventually, the school portfolio team compiles the registries in a binder as part of the school portfolio.

Artifacts and Evidence Registry

Briefly list here any artifacts and evidence that represent actions for the selected priority(ies).

Priority: *Literacy Instruction*

Samples of student writing portfolios

Assessments and individualized literacy plans

Videotape of student reading

Class stories generated by students

Copies of registries from various students' literacy portfolios, showing dates and visitors

Figure 5.8 Sample Artifacts and Evidence Registry

As the team members compile the school portfolio for display, they include action team priority information, along with a portfolio purpose statement at the beginning. They have a section in the school portfolio devoted to each priority. The priorities will vary from school to school, which is what makes the portfolio, a product constructed by a team for that particular school community, an authentic process.

As the team proceeds to the fourth and last step of the process, they use the So What? (Outcome) journal form (see Figure 5.9) to reflect on the ultimate goals and accomplishments of the school portfolio and learnings from the process.

School Portfolio Wrap-Up

Constructing a school portfolio is an opportunity for members of the school community to come together and discuss their priorities and progress in achieving their outcomes for student learning. The school leadership team, the parent organization, and site administrator(s) all have an opportunity to participate on the school portfolio team, as well as to collect, reflect, and select artifacts and evidence of student successes to feature in the school portfolio.

The school portfolio journal can assist portfolio team members in collecting artifacts for their

So What? (Outcome)

1. Prepare the final product (the school portfolio) to be displayed at the school site.

2. Each priority team will contribute descriptions of programs and practices as well as the purpose for each priority section in the school portfolio binder. Members will also include artifacts and evidence of priorities and future plans.

3. The portfolio will be exhibited to the entire school community and will continue to serve as a presentation or album portfolio for orientating new families to the school.

4. Each year the portfolio can be revisited and updates can be added to reflect the process of continual school improvement.

Figure 5.9 Sample Outcome

portfolio as they reaffirm their shared purpose, priorities, and outcomes for students in the community. When the portfolio is completed, it can serve as a hallmark album to be shared with others, a process that describes and illustrates the priorities, achievements, and future plans for the school.

Using the structured journal as a guide, the school portfolio process is easy to follow as you

- Begin with developing a shared *purpose*.

- Determine a *focus* or action priorities.

- Establish a *process* for collecting artifacts (evidence) that describe strategies and outcomes for action priorities, and represent a design for the portfolio.

- Exhibit the *outcome* and share the portfolio as a album of achievements and plans for the future of the school community.

Helpful Hints

Having a container for your collection of artifacts and evidences helps! Consider a zipper bag, big canvas bag, or a file-box with folders. As recommended, decide ahead of time—as a team—what form and design you want for the school portfolio, so that when each priority group comes together to compile the school portfolio, it flows like a storybook.

Reflection and Conversation

Using the School Portfolio Journal

1. The primary purpose and function of constructing our school portfolio . . .

2. How will we encourage key school community members to engage in the process?

3. How will we facilitate the process of bringing school community members together to define purpose and priorities?

4. Some creative ideas for artifacts that demonstrate achieving our priorities as a school community are . . .

5. How will we share the "product" with school community members and new comers?

6. How can we use learnings from the process to support on-going school improvement efforts?

Chapter 6

Study Group Journal

"School-wide study groups bring individual needs and institutional needs together in an organizational setting." (Murphy 1995, 38)

Background of Study Group

A study group provides a collaborative environment for teachers, administrators, other school staff, parents, and community members—with their varying backgrounds, knowledge, and skills—to come together to learn. It offers a learning environment for members who are interested in similar questions, topics, or specific concerns about the school community. In some districts, schoolwide study groups have been implemented. Their primary purpose is to focus the entire school community on exploring and considering educational practices that will result in an increase in student achievement.

Study groups can "stir" innovations to minimize or avoid the traditional compliance-implementation process. The group provides time for members to explore theoretical backgrounds and reflect on teaching practices, constructing a framework for thoughtfully planned innovation.

As an example of what the study group as a framework for change can accomplish, a group of teacher-leaders in a large urban school district recently formed a group to

- Assist in implementing curricular and instructional innovations.
- Develop school improvement plans.
- Give impetus to a focus on new educational theory and best practices in terms of teaching and learning.

How to Use the Study Group Journal

As with the other frameworks for change, the study group journal process involves four steps (Purpose, Focus, Process, and Outcome). Typically, the study group is comprised of the teacher-leaders who facilitate and direct the study groups at various school sites. The members of the study groups, drawn from throughout the school community, first meet to discuss the purpose of their particular study group and how they will work together.

Part of this phase involves determining how teachers will participate in the study group process, particularly if the outcomes of their work will be part of their professional evaluation. In the case of the study group mentioned previously—the one that serves as the focus of the Case Study in this chapter—the professional portfolio process had been used as an alternative teacher evaluation in the past. However, the school district decided the study group process might better meet the needs of the teacher leadership group.

As this study group met for the second session, it devoted time to determining a theme or topic for study and choosing the resources the members would employ, as well as, deciding what they wanted to learn. Using the journaling process, the participants reflected on the theory of multiple intelligences, new research in brain-compatible learning, and integrated curriculum design as possible entry points. After the themes were determined, the group selected books, articles, and multimedia resources for study and observation.

The next few meetings were sessions in which the learning community reflected on their readings and dialogued about their varying interpretations and understandings of what they had researched. These strategies are characteristic of the study group journaling process. The final session was devoted to presenting the outcome of the study group's work to peers and administrators, reflecting their work as facilitators for school change and professional growth.

The experience of this group is typical of the study group journaling process as it is used for optimum results.

Organization

The study group journal, being organized around the four steps of Purpose, Focus, Process, and Outcome, guides and facilitates the group in the chosen area of research and inquiry.

The study group members begin by clarifying what a study group is, why they are part of it, and what they would like to accomplish. Critical questions to address at this initial step are

- What is your primary purpose for participating in the study group?

- What will your group commitment be in terms of participation and contributions?

- What new understandings should come out of your study group's work?

Journal Process and Design

As with other frameworks for change, journaling facilitates collaboration and reflection. The journal forms in this chapter will assist in determining resources for reading and observation around the selected theme. Following is a template for the journaling process, including actions that characterize each step:

Why? (Purpose)

- Orientate yourself to the whole study group process.

- Determine why you are involved and what your goal is.

What If? (Focus)

- Identify the theme for study. Discuss specific interests, concerns, ideas for innovations, and target research areas that members of the group have in common.

- Establish a focus and decide on a resource(s) for study.

How Will It Work? (Process)

- Work together as a group to make a commitment to a study plan. Establish a schedule and study guide for your inquiry and learning.

- As you meet regularly throughout the process, be mindful that your study plan may be altered along the way, based upon new learnings that may be encountered.

So What? (Outcome)

- Participate in the final session by sharing reflections as you demonstrate, describe, and illustrate learnings, determining applications and implications for your professional work.

When the study group process is introduced, it is important that participants establish a shared (common) interest, such as a desire to read a particular book or to explore a plan for school restructuring. The Learning Cycle of Professional Development, a resource in the appendix of this book (see page 129), is useful background reading at this point.

Case Study: Study Group Journal

Following is an overview of the journaling process, including samples of journals and activities from actual study group experiences. When you are ready to apply the journaling process with your colleagues, note that blanks of the study group journal forms shown here are offered in the blacklines section (see pages 122–126). Commentary is provided before each sample form, explaining how the study group in this case applied the journaling process to facilitate this particular framework for change.

The questions in the first journal form (see Figure 6.1) involve initial observations and reflections by individual participants. Reflection and observation are strategies integral to the Purpose step of the process.

Why? (Purpose)

1. What are you currently observing in your professional work that is related to your interests and/or concerns as an educator?

   In my school community, it seems that there is a growing conflict between a traditional top-down approach to managing our work and a growing need to move into a shared-leadership, community-based environment. With so many changes and new research regarding education, I feel a need to explore options for changing how we work with our students and how we balance professional learning with accountability.

2. What would you like to know more about or be able to do differently in your professional practice?

   I would like to know more about learning communities and how they might exist in our schools. How we can introduce that thinking into our school community and still meet the demands of standards and assessments?

3. What are your personal theories about what the purpose of education will be in the twentieth-first century?

   I think the purpose has expanded and we now take on responsibilities for things schools never were responsible for in the past. We have created a generation of "school-dependent children" and we have possibly taken on more than we can manage. The purpose of education is to support and then facilitate the development of a child, so that the child can have a meaningful, purposeful life and live as a responsible, independent adult. It is occurring to me that this is a tall order and one that must be mediated by relationship-building in the school community.

Figure 6.1 Sample Purpose

As the study group journaling process continues, the group is mindful of the four steps (Purpose, Focus, Process, and Outcome), but works on focusing the inquiry and listing resources, using the What If? (Focus) journal form (see Figure 6.2) for personal reflection and to establish a research target. At this point, the group members establish parameters for time and participation. It is important to realize that the learning of each study group member is dependent on the energy and commitment of their colleagues.

What If? (Focus)

1. We have selected _____ to be the core resource for our study group because . . .

   We chose Assessment In the Learning Organization: Shifting the Paradigm edited by Arthur L. Costa and Bena Kallick because we are concerned about the balance between professional learning and accountability. The book has theoretical background ideas as well as chapters contributed by professional educators out in the field doing the work!

2. Additional resources we might employ as part of our study are . . .

   Articles that support some of our specific assessment needs and, possibly, visits to a school site nearby that has been doing study groups for several years.

3. How is our study group inquiry connected to my current teaching practices and professional needs?

   The new push for national and local standards is putting a great deal of pressure on us. We are trying to avoid another hoop to jump through, or another checklist. In order to do this, teachers will have to be involved in the planning process at a new level. We are looking for a process to make learning part of our daily work to stay in the rapid flow of change in terms of school community needs.

Figure 6.2 Sample Focus

At this point, it is important to facilitate the conversation that moves the group from the Purpose and Focus steps to the generation of essential questions for study. Using the How Will It Work? (Process) journal form (see Figure 6.3), the group begins the journey fully aware that the essential question for study may shift during the Process step. However, the members note it is important to agree at the outset on a study plan structure and to reach an agreement if change is needed.

How Will It Work? (Process)

Theme of Study Plan

Assessment in the Learning Organization: Shifting the Paradigm

Themes for our discussions will include...

Session I

Essential question:

What are the purpose, meaning, and function of assessment in the teaching-learning process? (Book source: Introduction and Chapter 1)

Session II

Essential question:

Why are learning communities vital for systemic change in our educational systems? (Book source)

Session III

Essential question:

How can we identify, establish, and sustain learning communities? (Book source: "Seven Tasks Facing Learning Organizations," pp. 213–221)

Session IV

Essential question:

How can we build trusting relationships to move toward commitment for continuous improvement? (Book source: "Teams Build Assessment and Assessment Builds Teams," pp. 141–152)

Session V

Essential question:

What have others done to establish an environment where assessment and feedback are invited and encouraged? And what does it mean to self-assess? (Book source: "Feedback Spirals as Components of Continued Learning," pp. 25–29)

Session VI

Outcome, reflections, implications, and conclusions:

We will determine these later.

Figure 6.3 Sample Process

SkyLight Training and Publishing Inc.

The study group uses the Checkpoint journal form (see Figure 6.4) to capture reflections during the process and take notes for future sharing on the essential question for each session.

Going to the fourth step of the study group journaling process, the group members individually reflect on the Outcome of their study, using the So What? (Outcome) journal form (Figure 6.5).

Checkpoint

Date: *February 15*

Session: *IV*

I am observing . . .

that trusting relationships are lacking in my school community.

I am learning . . .

that relationships are key to systemic school change.

Resources I have discovered . . .

a school in our county that has implemented schoolwide study groups to help build community partnerships and collaborative relationships.

Questions I am asking . . .

How can we determine the readiness of our school community to make a commitment to change?

Figure 6.4 Sample Checkpoint

So What? (Outcome)

CONCLUSIONS, REFLECTIONS, ADAPTATIONS, MODIFICATIONS, AND LEARNINGS

As a result of participating in the study group, I learned a great deal about the concept of learning organization and how that might apply to our school community. I also learned that we do not currently honor learning or learning by experience for professional educators. My concern is that if we want that to become a norm in our school community—the learning community process needs to start with us.

It was also interesting to listen to my colleagues and realize that we share many concerns and perspectives and that, as a result of our exploration and learning in this study group, we might just have the critical mass to start looking differently at our school programs and students.

The concern of assessment is still breathing down our backs as we face standards. The process of learning community needs to grow, develop, and evolve. It is about who you are—not just what you do; it will take time and we have little time to respond to assessment demands. The challenge will be to identify future steps to keep our journey to learn alive.

What articulating, sharing, demonstrating, and exhibiting do you plan to do with peers in regard to your learnings?

So far I have shared the progress of our group at a staff meeting at my school. I am hoping that next term we can have another group from the staff go through the study group process for the same book, with possibly one of our group acting as a facilitator to get the new study group started.

(continued on next page)

What new questions about the process have emerged from your participation in the study group?
The study group is a powerful process. It does demand commitment—it is so easy to say I am too busy to go. It is like saying I am too busy to learn. That does not make sense for a professional educator!

What have you learned about yourself as a learner?
I learned how important the social/collaborative process is to learning. Without a group commitment, I would never have read a book on learning organizations or had the level of reflection and connections to my work that I now have. It was a reminder of the damage isolation can do to educators and the entire school community.

What are the implications of your learnings on your professional work?
We need to remind ourselves as educators that we are part of a learning organiza-tion and that community is a critical aspect of our work. I hope our study group can expand our circle of understanding over time, in order to facilitate a learning com-munity at our school.

Figure 6.5 Sample Outcome

Study Group Wrap-Up

"Learning is the continual structuring and restructuring of ideas though interaction with people, objects and ideas." (Grennon-Brooks 1996, 4**)**

Schoolwide study groups have been a powerful tool for change in schools. The concept of a study group approach has brought school communities together, expanding their collective understand-ing about a shared purpose and a commitment to professional learning. Offering a process for restructuring understandings and building a knowledge base related to professional growth, the study group serves as a useful framework for school change.

Using the structured journal as a guide, the study group process is easy to follow as you

- Establish a *purpose* for your research.
- Identify a *focus*.
- Design a plan and *process* for research.
- Move your plan into *action*.
- Reflect on the *outcome* of your study.
- *Revise* teaching practices, as indicated by your research, and work toward systemic school change.

Helpful Hints

When your study group meets for the first time, set dates for check-points—regular meetings to discuss learnings. Make a commitment from the beginning and stick to the dates. This will reinforce the responsibility teachers have to be learners.

Reflection and Conversation

Opportunities for Using a Study Group

1. I would like to understand why my students seem to consistently have difficulty with . . .

2. What studies have been completed that deal with . . .

3. What would the impact on student learning be if I . . .

4. How could we incorporate study group and research efforts into the current teacher evaluation process?

5. What are the benefits of having a study group in our school system?

6. How can we better schedule meeting times for sharing reflections?

Blacklines

Guides
and
Resources

Guide for Professional Collaboration

Constructivist collaboration is the action and interaction among willing participants that results in learning. It usually involves a combination of talking, listening, observing, doing, thinking, and reflecting. Collaboration can have a variety of purposes and is often initiated by a specific focus or need. The process of collaboration may lead to discovering new understandings, purposes, and needs.

How does collaboration differ from simple discussion? The primary difference is the purpose for the conversation. A collaboration would be a dialogue fueled by exploring an issue, in which questions such as What if? How about? or Why? are posed—thus inviting new thinking and creativity. A discussion, on the other hand, would be a conversation that examines the pros and cons of a known quantity or fact.

Consider the purposes, processes, and outcomes of peer collaborations:

To discover

Listen to understand.   Talk to listen.

Listen to pose questions.   Talk to explain or clarify.

To invent

Listen to focus.   Talk to interpret.

Guide for Professional Collaboration *(cont.)*

To plan

Listen to empathize.   Talk to invite reflection.

Listen to rethink.   Do to discover.

Some examples of collaboration as a combination of interactions, actions, and purposes are

Reflective Conversations

These conversations often include responses and interactions that help to clarify, summarize, focus, and hypothesize, as well as invite rethinking.

Critical Friend Conversations

These interactions are usually with colleagues or other individuals with whom you have a high level of trust, and with whom you can openly reflect, give and receive feedback, and restructure thinking.

Sharing and Supporting Conversations

These are opportunities to openly share emotions as well as receive acceptance and support. These conversations are usually initiated by sharing reactions and feelings related to a specific event or topic.

Roundtable or Debriefing

These conversations are aimed at communicating learning, re-thinking, hypothesizing, and/or generating ideas directly related to an observed activity(ies).

Banner Questions Guide

Sample Banner Questions

Would student learning be enhanced if there were opportunities for creative exploration of individual interests/talents?

How do I construct a thinking-meaning-centered curriculum for all students that addresses the needs of all learners?

How can I move away from letter grading/effort grading systems to one that communicates students' specific accomplishments?

What causes children to be aggressive and strike out at other children?

What are the various kinds of creative learning environments that provide less fragmentation and more integration between skill and content?

How can I effectively integrate evaluation and assessment for successful and useful program evaluation?

How can I meet the needs of "academically challenged" students and—at the same time—meet the needs of my "top" students?

Why do seventh grade students get "off track" so easily when they move to a departmentalized, rotating schedule?

What motivates eighth grade students?

Why is there such a difference between oral and written communication?

How can I make learning relevant to high school students?

How can we define or redefine academic rigor?

Your Banner Question:

Banner Questions Guide (cont.)

Splinter Questions:

How does your banner question relate to your work?

What do you hope to learn?

Who are your collaborator(s), partner(s), or study group teammate(s)?

What resources and learning opportunities are you considering?

Professional Development Checklist

"The traditional approach to helping educators learn has been to develop the skills of individuals to do their work. Staff development needs to enhance the collective capacity of people to create and pursue overall visions." (Senge 1994, **9**)

Portfolio Checkpoints for Building a Learning Community

Purpose

√ Introduce portfolio purpose and process.

√ Formulate and share your professional credo.

√ Discuss issues, concerns, and interests.

Focus

√ Establish and share banner questions.

√ Ask structured interview questions.

√ Discuss splinter questions related to the priority.

Process

√ Identify "entry points" for learning using reflective collaboration.

√ Collect and reflect on learning activities.

√ Share artifacts and evidence.

Outcome

√ Share, reflect, and rethink.

√ Describe learnings.

√ Demonstrate and celebrate.

Professional Portfolios
Types and Purposes

Presentation Portfolio

A collection, resume, or album that represents an individual's accomplishments, learnings, strengths, and expertise. It can serve as an introduction for personal and professional opportunities—highlighting the purpose and meaning of one's work.

Working Portfolio

A collection of assignments, artifacts, and evidence that fulfill prescribed competencies, standards, or outcomes. Outcomes for credentialing, course participation, or other requirements established by mediators, teachers, or supervisors of one's work may be included.

Learner Portfolio

"An envelope of the mind" that provides a framework and process for *learner-centered decisions* and designs—connecting the learner's goals and purposes with those of his or her work.

Guide to Reflection on Professional Growth

Reflection into Action

Refection into Practice

The thoughtful questions below are based on

- Portfolio inquiry

- Observations

- Learning activities

- Previous conversations

- Crisis at hand

Can you talk more about that?

Why do you think that happens?

What evidence do you have about that?

What does this remind you of?

Do you see a connection between this and anything else you have done before?

How else could you approach that?

What do you want to happen?

How could you do that?

What is your plan?

Note: These "thoughtful questions" are adapted from Christine Canning's "What Teachers Say About Reflection," *Educational Leadership* (March 1991): 18–21.

Student Profile Checklist

Questions for Evaluators to Ask

1. What do we predict will be the skills, abilities, knowledge base, and attitudes that all students will need to be successful and fulfilled in the future?

2. What academic and behavioral outcomes should we be striving to instill in our students?

3. What should our priorities be in creating a learning environment to achieve these outcomes?

4. What specialized skills, attitudes, values, or abilities should our school programs include?

5. What do we view as the most important characteristics of a school that is devoted to both "rigor and relevance"?

Directions for Coaching Triads

Form triads (group of three) for purposes of collaborative listening and select roles for the first round. Complete three rounds during one session so each triad member will have an opportunity to experience all three roles listed below.

Role of Storyteller

Talks about the focus of learning for professional growth. Tells about experiences and observations that prompted interest and/ or questions.

Examples of activities that might have prompted learning include observations (an individual's class and/or other classes); seminars or workshops; videotapes; conversations with colleagues, parents, or students; readings; and samples of student work.

Role of Listener

Listens at three levels: to hear ideas and details; to hear in order to pose questions; to hear in order to understand.

The listener is careful not to interrupt thinking on the part of the storyteller, asking questions only to clarify understanding. The listener's major function is to "coach" the storyteller and assist that person in clarifying the process—in order to focus on a target area, to take action, or to resolve misunderstandings.

Role of Observer

Listens to the conversation and notes the process used by both the listener and the storyteller.

The observer takes notes regarding specific techniques he or she noticed. When the listening session for a round is complete, the observer offers feedback to the listener and to the storyteller.

A List of Facilitation Strategies

Jigsaw: Process for reading, summarizing, and integrating text.

Each participant reads a portion of the text, shares information, and collects information from others as well.

Carousel: Design for collecting ideas, reactions, and suggestions surrounding a model, strategic plan, or event.

Post charts around the room; write responses, suggestions, observations, and ideas; then walk around to read, respond, and enhance comments.

Multimedia Metaphor: Catalyst for constructing, connecting, and comparing multiple frames of reference.

Show brief video clip or read literature selection to facilitate dialogue regarding the representational meaning in the metaphor.

Cut Story: Technique for reading aloud—as a "team" or with the entire group.

Paste text on index cards; then hand out the cards and have the group assemble in the appropriate order. Read the message aloud to the rest of the group.

Consulting Line: Design for aligning and connecting expertise with problems in the room.

Have participants line up in two rows facing each other. Ask the persons on the left to share a concern or problem they are experiencing. Have the corresponding partners on the right act as consultants and offer suggestions, solutions, pose questions, etc. After about five minutes, have each consultant on the right move to the next person in line and interview that person. As the line moves, each person meets another consultant and gains additional suggestions and questions. After two or three rounds, have the persons on the left become the consultants. Repeat this cycle several times.

A List of Facilitation Strategies

(Cont.)

Walk the Talk: Pick a partner and take a walk.

Select a topic, problem, or essential question. Report back at a specified time to share conversations with the others. This activity provides an opportunity to take a break, move around, and collaborate.

Visual Dialogue: Tool for collecting and recording the learnings in the room.

This tool could be graphic organizer such as a mind map, a web, a drawing, a list, a chart, etc. Have a recorder keep a log of the session for the group.

Fish Bowl: Group dynamics technique for listening to others.

While others look on to observe, summarize, and take notes, inner-circle members of a group respond to essential questions.

Think-Pair-Share: Process for reflecting, writing, and sharing.

People pair up and compare thoughts with others in the room.

Constructive Controversy: A process for engaging in conversation.

Selecting a controversial issue, group members express as well as listen to multiple points of view.

A Guide for Listening

Levels of Listening

Level 1   Listen *to* sort information.

Focused on understanding

Level 2   Listen *for* themes, categories, clusters of ideas.

Focused on identifying speaker's needs

Level 3   Listen *with* metaview (with the "big picture" in mind).

Foused on needs, priorities, and commitment to action for the speaker

Conscious listening is being 100% present for the speaker.

Thoughtful Questions for Learning Communities

Below are eight thoughtful questions that are useful when working with

- Action research teams

- Professional portfolio "roundtables"

- School/district leadership teams

- School improvement committees

- Study groups

For each question below, fill in the blank with the group's selected focus or priority.

- How does _____ impact student learning?

- How can _____ contribute to self-esteem?

- What evidence/experience do we have that _____ is important to the educational process?

- How might _____ change what you are doing?

- What are the implementation considerations for the proposed change?

- What capacities, understandings, and commitments are necessary to consider _____?

- What are the willingness and the readiness levels among staff members for considering _____?

- What are your suggestions regarding the proposal or issue?

Worksheet for Defining Purpose and Priorities

Agreement regarding the purpose, or being aligned in terms of common purpose and desired outcome, is a critical starting point. It builds the foundation for effective design and implementation of school change efforts. Change efforts work best when shared purpose and priorities are clearly agreed upon from the beginning.

Such alignment provides

- the context for decision making

- the yardstick for progress

- the focus for collaboration and shared responsibility

- the motivator for excellence and high performance

****

Following are leading questions for defining shared purpose and establishing schoolwide priorities:

1. From my perspective, the primary purpose for schooling . . .

2. I see my major contributions to the school community as being . . .

3. I will consider our change efforts worthwhile if the following things happen . . .

School Portfolio Survey

Reflect on and discuss the following statements, deciding whether you agree (A) or disagree (D) with them.

1. School portfolios contain collections of artifacts and evidence representing growth and learning.

2. The portfolio process is so engaging that everyone catches on and is eager to participate from the start.

3. Checkpoints and feedback loops, designed to assess progress and refocus directions, are important to document in the school portfolio process.

4. Once there is agreement on the purpose and process for school change, the school portfolio framework should be easy to implement.

5. The school portfolio is essentially a scrapbook that tells a story.

6. School portfolios should come to a close at the end of each school term.

7. The school portfolio design, process, contents, and outcome will vary according to the purpose of the school portfolio.

8. The first step in designing a school portfolio is to collect data and then establish a purpose for the portfolio.

9. The portfolio process can enhance school and community involvement in the change process.

10. A rubric really drives the portfolio process.

The school portfolio group should work toward consensus as they take this survey. (See page 128 for the recommended answers.)

A Strategy for Determining Top Priorities for School Change

Purpose

To identify top priorities for improving student performance schoolwide and to determine priorities for goal-setting for the school community.

Process

Step 1: Outline the purpose, process, and payoff (outcome) for the school portfolio process session by presenting an overview of a session. This is a prime opportunity to discuss the importance of community involvement. It is also a good time to establish a focus or "entry point" for school improvement. (Recommended time: five minutes.)

Step 2: Divide into smaller groups, five to eight persons in each. They may be formed according interests or schools, or members may be randomly selected. Have the small groups address the following task:

> Brainstorm what your top priorities are for school improvement/change, such as literacy, technology, interpersonal skills, block scheduling, etc.

The groups should record their data on flip chart paper. (Recommended time: fifteen minutes.)

Step 3: The data are condensed into one specific list of priorities for all the groups. (This list may have ten to twenty items.) (Recommended time: five minutes.)

(continued on next page)

A Strategy for Determining Top Priorities for School Change
(cont.)

Step 4: With participants having compiled a condensed list of priorities for the entire school portfolio group, they now vote. Have participants prepare a numbered list on a master sheet of paper. Each number corresponds with one priority.

Each participant may vote three times for any three, any two, or just one of the items. Participants mark the list next to the selected item to indicate their votes. If one item in particular is a concern for them, they may choose to put three marks on one line, or two on one, and one on another, and so on. The greatest number of votes per item determines the top priorities for school change. (Recommended time: five minutes.)

Step 5: The results are immediate and provide the school community with a fair scan of the opinion on top priorities for school change efforts.

TThe group now can determine the readiness, structure, and "entry point" for designing an improvement (action) plan. It is important to keep in mind that not all items on the priority list will be addressed at the same time, and that the beginning point does not necessarily mean that other concerns will be neglected. (Recommended time: ten minutes.)

Payoff

Determining two or three priorities (areas) for goal-setting for the school community.

Blacklines

Journal Forms

Why? (Purpose)

OBSERVATIONS · CONCERNS · QUESTIONS

- Why do you want to form this action research group?

- How long will you work together?

- How will you collaborate and take action on learnings?

The action research journal provides a framework for identifying, planning, and facilitating research. It provides opportunities for

1. Identifying a target area for research.

2. Building a research plan.

3. Collecting information.

4. Collaborating with peers as research partners.

5. Observing.

6. Assessing impact of strategies used in target area.

7. Refining practices.

8. Reflecting on experiences.

Purpose Statement . . .

Fig. 2.1 (Action Research Journal) © 1998 SkyLight Training and Publishing Inc.

Observations

1. What are your observations regarding student learning?

2. Describe strategies and practices that have been effective and others that have not worked so well.

3. What are your interests and concerns about your work?

What If? (Focus)

BANNER QUESTIONS

- What do you need to know?

- What are you especially interested in?

- What do you wonder about?

- What are some of your concerns?

Research team establishes a research target.

Research Focus Discussion

Research Target

I. Action Questions

What if . . .

How about . . .

How could I . . .

II. Collegial Connections

III. Strategies and Skills to Implement

Our goal is . . .

We need to address . . .

Fig. 2.4 (Action Research Journal)   © 1998 SkyLight Training and Publishing Inc.

How Will It Work? (Process)

PLAN · DATA COLLECTION · COLLABORATION

- When will you meet?

- How will you collect data?

- What process will you use for observations and information gathering?

- How will you share roles and responsibilities in the group?

PLAN · ACT · REFLECT · REVISE

Research Plan

- Strategies to be employed

- Implementation plan

- Data collection template

- Observations and reflective collaborations

- Refinements of the plan

Fig. 2.5 (Action Research Journal)   © 1998 SkyLight Training and Publishing Inc.

Research Plan (Strategy)

Preparation

Materials:

Methods:

Resources:

Implementation Schedule

Fig. 2.6 (Action Research Journal)

Data Collection Form

Collecting and Analyzing Multiple Sources of Data to Study the Impact of Action Plans

WHO (demographic data to be collected)

Number of Students:

Gender: M _____ F _____

Stable student population (over 3 years):

Attendance:

Other:

HOW (processing of data and strategies in research plan)

SO WHAT (outcomes-formal and informal data)

Other Outcomes

Surveys

Fig. 2.7 (Action Research Journal)   © 1998 SkyLight Training and Publishing Inc.

So What? (Outcome)

OBSERVATIONS, LEARNINGS, REFINEMENTS, ACTIONS

- How has your research impacted your work as an educator?

- How will you communicate findings?

- What actions will you take?

CONCLUSIONS, REFLECTIONS, RETHINKING, AND LEARNINGS

What hypotheses did you bring to your research target area?

How did the data collection support your learning?

What new questions have emerged from your research?

Fig. 2.8 (Action Research Journal)   © 1998 SkyLight Training and Publishing Inc.

Why? (Purpose)

OBSERVATIONS · CONCERNS · QUESTIONS

- What is the purpose of the journal for professional growth/ the professional portfolio?

The professional growth journal/professional portfolio will provide opportunities for us to

1. Focus our professional development.

2. Build and adapt a learning plan.

3. Collect artifacts and evidence.

4. Collaborate with peers, as partners and in groups.

5. Sharpen professional management skills.

6. Apply leadership abilities.

7. Draw on past experiences and knowledge.

8. Observe and contribute to collegial development.

9. Assess the impact and influence of systemic change in our school.

10. Reflect on values, attitudes, and experiences.

Fig. 3.1 (Professional Growth Journal)   © 1998 SkyLight Training and Publishing Inc.

Descriptions of Learning Opportunities

Focus Development
Identify an "entry point" for professional growth. Select an area of concern, interest, and/or expertise that is a priority for you and articulate it in the form of a banner question—a leading question.

Build and Adapt a Learning Plan
Select learning activities that contribute to your learning (inquiry) process. Choose activities that can provide a variety of experiences and highlight interactions with individuals and ideas.

Collect Artifacts and Evidence
Gather data and items for portfolios that represent development and reflect new understandings in terms of professional growth.

Collaborate With Peers as Partners and in Groups
Meet with a portfolio partner on an ongoing basis and in roundtable discussion groups with other participants in the learning community. Roundtable discussions may include colleagues who have similar learning priorities, consultants, and members of the school administration/school community who are involved in the process.

Sharpen Management Skills
Identify skills that may be involved with your banner question, choosing from the standard professional skills that help you "get the job done."

(cont. on next page)

Fig. 3.2 (Professional Growth Journal)   © 1998 SkyLight Training and Publishing Inc.

Descriptions of Learning Opportunities (cont.)

Applying Leadership Abilities
Choosing from those features that are characteristic of effective leadership, identify abilities that are connected to professional growth and the portfolio process.

Draw on Past Experiences and Knowledge
Consider prior learnings and use them as a starting point for your inquiry, as you form your banner question and build a learning plan with your portfolio partner.

Observe and Contribute to Collegial Development
Create an environment in which every person is a teacher and every teacher a learner. (Throughout the journaling/portfolio process, you will have opportunities to collaborate and be both a learner and a teacher.)

Assess the Impact of Your Work on School Systems
Consider the systems within your school community that will support or interfere with the outcome of this professional portfolio process.

Reflect on Values, Attitudes, and Experiences
Meet with peers and, as a group, reflect in your journals on learning activities and classroom practices, selecting artifacts and evidence for inclusion in the process.

Defining Your Professional Credo

I.   What are your beliefs about the purpose of your profession?

II.   Describe the ideal curriculum.

III.   What are your beliefs about how students learn?

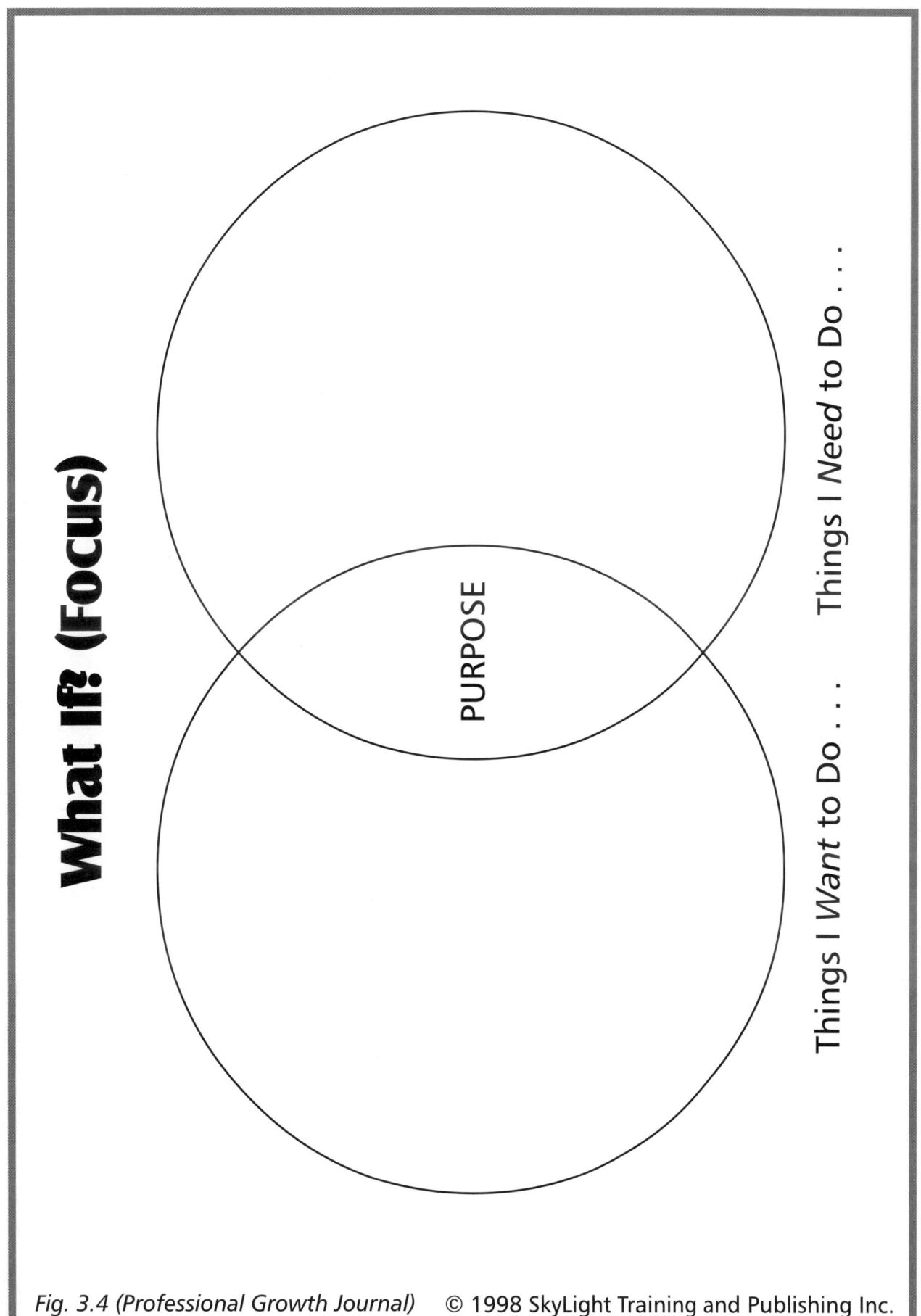

What If? (Focus)

PURPOSE

Things I *Need* to Do . . . .

Things I *Want* to Do . . . .

Fig. 3.4 (Professional Growth Journal) © 1998 SkyLight Training and Publishing Inc.

Banner Question

Splinter Questions

How Will It Work? (Process)

PLAN • DATA COLLECTION • COLLABORATION

- Make professional growth and development plans.

- Collect artifacts and evidence as part of the portfolio process.

- Participate in professional development activities.

- Establish points to cover for next meeting.

Professional Development Plan

Focusing on the development of a plan, you establish collaborations to facilitate and support learning. Your professional development activities should be selected in terms of your individual classroom teaching situations and the context of your banner questions.

The plan will contain your

1. Credo

2. Banner question

3. Professional development activities

4. Outcome, as well as any "re-thinkings" and applications to professional/classroom practices

(cont. on next page)

Fig. 3.6 (Professional Growth Journal) © 1998 SkyLight Training and Publishing Inc.

How Will It Work? (Process)

(cont.)

The professional development plan will facilitate perusal and integrate learning from the inquiry. Begin with activities you are *currently involved in.* Continue to add activities to your plan as you move through the portfolio process and collaborate with others.

Some examples of professional development activities are

- Visiting other schools

- Attending seminars

- Observing teaching and group facilitation activities in progress

- Meeting with other educators who share your interests

- Inviting a colleague to observe you at a meeting or professional workshop

- Reading articles from professional journals

- Joining a study group in the school community

- Researching a theme or concept related to your banner question

Fig. 3.6 cont. (Professional Growth Journal) © 1998 SkyLight Training and Publishing Inc.

Professional Development Log

Month   Activity

Collaborations

When you meet with your colleagues during this stage of the professional growth journaling/portfolio process, reflect on your daily decisions and other experiences related to your inquiry. Discuss the integration and connections among the standards for your profession and if you are "aligned on purpose"—that is, if you have defined a common purpose for your work.

To facilitate collaboration. . .

- Discuss issues.

- Focus on banner question.

- Consider professional development activities.

- Discuss recent experiences.

- Share your professional development plan.

- Plan to observe and/or meet with a partner.

- Ask for feedback or input regarding a decision.

- Make adaptations to your professional development plan.

- Ask for suggestions regarding activities for your plan.

- Exhibit artifacts and/or evidence from your portfolio.

- Share current findings or learnings.

Fig. 3.8 (Professional Growth Journal)   © 1998 SkyLight Training and Publishing Inc.

Artifacts and Evidence Registry

Briefly list below any artifacts and evidence, gathered for your professional portfolio, that prompt reflection or collaboration in relation to your banner question.

So What? (Outcome)

DEMONSTRATE • ARTICULATE • EXHIBIT LEARNINGS

Reflections, Rethinking, Conclusions, and Learnings

What articulation, sharing, demonstrating, and exhibiting have you done in regard to your professional portfolio?

What new questions have emerged from your inquiry and development?

How have your beliefs or practices been challenged or changed?

A possible future banner question?

Fig. 3.10 (Professional Growth Journal) © 1998 SkyLight Training and Publishing Inc.

Why? (Purpose)

1. Describe the role of teacher as facilitator of student learning.

2. What do you see as the primary purpose of the staff development?

3. What are your personal theories about how children learn?

What If? (Focus)

1. The instructional area I have chosen in which to apply learnings from this staff development is . . .

2. The staff development will alter my current practices, since . . .

Will It Work? (Process)

Date:
Session:

I expected . . .   I learned . . .

I plan to use . . .   Next time . . .

So What? (Outcome)

CONCLUSIONS, REFLECTIONS, ADAPTATIONS, MODIFICATIONS, LEARNINGS

- What articulating, sharing, demonstrating and exhibiting have you done with your peers in regard to your learnings?

- What new questions about your study and strategies have emerged from participation in the staff development?

- How have your beliefs about student needs changed?

- Future plans for using the new practices should include . . .

Fig. 4.4 (Staff Development Journal)   © 1998 SkyLight Training and Publishing Inc.

Portfolio

School Name

School Portfolio Team

Names of team members

_____

_____

_____

_____

_____

_____

_____

_____

Fig. 5.1 (School Portfolio Journal)   © 1998 SkyLight Training and Publishing Inc.

Guide for Defining Purpose

The school portfolio is an organizer for planning and reflecting on continuous school improvement. It is a framework for working together to identify school priorities and exhibit student learning outcomes.

The school portfolio process provides a structure for

- Facilitating change.

- Working together as a staff and school community.

- Organizing, planning, and assessing student outcomes.

- Collecting artifacts and evidence.

- Building community relationships.

- Reflecting on values and attitudes.

- Drawing on past experiences and knowledge.

- Exploring possibilities.

- Building new understandings about priorities.

To work toward defining a purpose, the school portfolio team members will

1. Consider their definition of common purpose and formulate and share their philosophy, highlighting belief systems about the purpose and process of education.

2. Learn about the portfolio process as a tool for organizing school planning.

3. Build communication abilities and listening skills.

Fig. 5.2 (School Portfolio Journal) © 1998 SkyLight Training and Publishing Inc.

Why? (Purpose)

1. From my perspective the primary indicators of student learning are . . .

2. My personal theory about how students learn is . . .

3. At our school I am most proud of . . .

Fig. 5.3 (School Portfolio Journal)   © 1998 SkyLight Training and Publishing Inc.

What If? (Focus)

At the Focus phase of the process, the school portfolio team will

1. Define the priorities for the school community.

2. Select the top six or eight priorities using the Action Priority Wheel (Figure 5.5).

3. Form priority work groups accordingly.

Ideally, each priority work group is a mixture of parents, teachers, and other school community members. The teachers can check in with colleagues regarding the collections of artifacts and program descriptions. The parents and other members can enhance the process with their various perspectives. The process of conversations and collaborations within these groups builds school community.

Action Priority Wheel

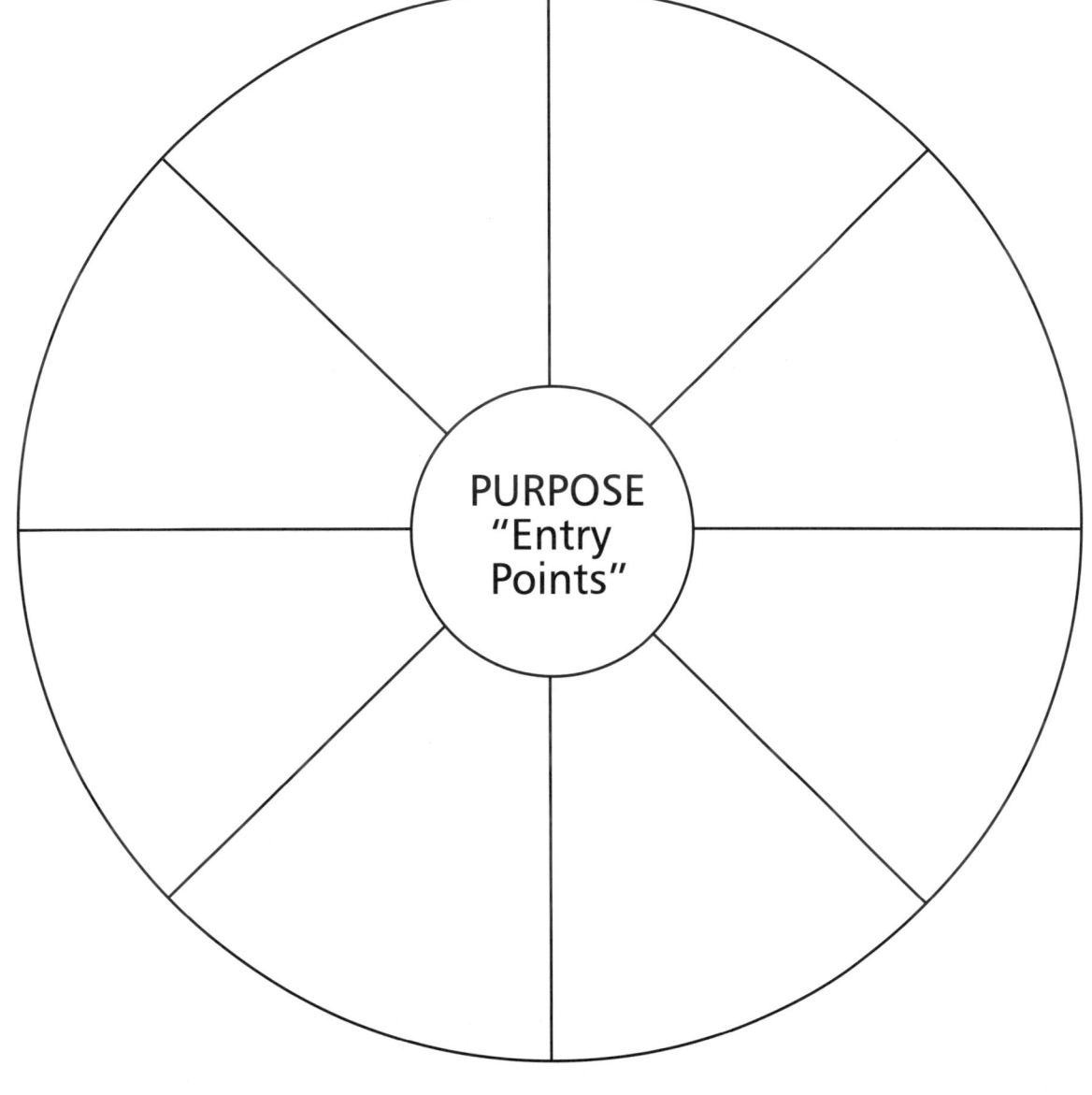

PURPOSE
"Entry
Points"

Fig. 5.5 (School Portfolio Journal)

How Will It Work? (Process)

At the process phase, the team will

1. Agree on a design and format for the school portfolio.

2. Meet with community members in their individual priority action teams.

3. Identify existing and future programs and practices that contribute to the various priorities.

4. Consider future programs and practices to support priorities for change.

5. Describe impact of existing programs.

6. Collect artifacts and evidence of accomplishments.

7. Agree on a plan for checkpoints (meetings to ascertain progress), as well as a time line for completion of the school portfolio.

Fig. 5.6 (School Portfolio Journal)

Priority Action Team Worksheet

Priority Description

Current Accomplishments

Future Plans and Suggestions

Artifacts and Evidence Registry

Briefly list any artifacts and evidence that represent actions for the selected priority(ies).

Priority:

So What? (Outcome)

1. Prepare the final product (school portfolio) to be displayed at the school site.

2. Each priority team will contribute descriptions of programs and practices as well as purpose for each priority section in the binder. Members will also include artifacts and evidence of priorities and future plans.

3. The portfolio will be exhibited to the entire school community and will continue to serve as a presentation or album portfolio for orientating new families to the school.

4. Each year the portfolio can be revisited and updates can be added to reflect the process of continual school improvement.

Fig. 5.9 (School Portfolio Journal)   © 1998 SkyLight Training and Publishing Inc.

Why? (Purpose)

1. What are you currently observing in your professional work that is related to your interests and/or concerns as an educator?

2. What would you like to know more about or be able to do differently in your professional practice?

3. What are your personal theories about what the purpose of education will be in the twenty-first century?

Fig. 6.1 (Study Group Journal)

What If? (Focus)

1. We have selected _____ to be the core resource for our study group because . . .

2. Additional resources we might employ as part of our study are . . .

3. How is our study group inquiry connected to my current practices and professional needs?

Fig. 6.2 (Study Group Journal)   © 1998 SkyLight Training and Publishing Inc.

How Will It Work? (Process)

Theme of Study Plan

Themes for our discussions will include . . .

Session I
Essential question:

Session II
Essential question:

Session III
Essential question:

Session IV
Essential question:

Session V
Essential question:

Session VI
Outcome, reflections, implications, and conclusions:

Checkpoint

Date:

Session:

I am observing . . .

I am learning . . .

Resources I have discovered . . .

Questions I am asking . . .

Fig. 6.4 (Study Group Journal)   © 1998 SkyLight Training and Publishing Inc.

So What? (Outcome)

CONCLUSIONS, REFLECTIONS, ADAPTATIONS, MODIFICATIONS, AND LEARNINGS

What articulating, sharing, demonstrating, and exhibiting do you plan to do with peers in regard to your learnings?

What new questions about the process have emerged from your participation in the study group?

What have you learned about yourself as a learner?

What are the implications of your learnings on your professional work?

Appendix

Answer key for School Portfolio Survey (on page 83)

Recommended answers: 1. A; 2. D; 3. A; 4. D; 5. A; 6. D; 7. A; 8. D; 9. A; 10. D.

The Learning Cycle of Professional Development

Teachers Constructing Conceptual Understandings

Using a constructivist approach to teacher development allows teachers to experience the type of learning environment they are expected to create for their students. There are two tools that are helpful in focusing and facilitating this process: the Learning Cycle for Teacher Development and the Learner-Centered Coaching Model, both organized and facilitated by the professional development portfolio process.

The combination of these models allow teacher-learners to (1) clarify the purpose, meaning, and function of their work; (2) focus their learnings based on interests, concerns, and needs; (3) identify their current level of expertise regarding their focus for learning; (4) select an "entry point" for learning; (5) seek the appropriate coaching (collaboration) activities to support and facilitate their professional growth; (6) continually reflect on and self-assess their learnings; and (7) describe, demonstrate, illustrate, or exhibit their rethinkings and learning outcomes.

This process can be used for beginning teachers and their mentors/coaches, or to support, in general, the professional development program for all teachers and their supervisors.

The Learning Cycle Model

The translation of learning theory into cycles of professional development is the foundation for the Learning Cycle Model. This model describes the pathway for continuous learning as teachers expand and deepen their understanding of the concepts and practices used in their profession. It helps teachers make informed decisions about appropriate learning plans for desired outcomes. Focusing learning in an effort to build conceptual understanding, the Learning Cycle Model assists teacher-learners in making connections among theories, practices, and their teaching experiences.

Judging by observation, research, and experience, it appears that teachers do pass through continuous learning cycles. These cycles are defined by four basic levels of development.

- *Exploration.* Teacher-learners are initially explorers, inquiring about a specific focus or priority. They are learning the territory, assessing information, observing students, listening to others, reading about theories, discovering new ideas, and exploring options and professional learning opportunities. Working with a mentor or coach, teacher-learners mediate their exploration by providing suggestions about professional development activities, asking questions, and sharing experiences.

- *Organization.* Teacher-learners observe as they (a) label things; (b) practice routines, procedures, and strategies; (c) clarify responses; and (d) recognize pedagogy and learning theories in their teaching environment. Representing what they have been observing and striving for, teacher-learners are prompted to place ideas in a sequence, accommodating and assimilating the data they have collected.

- *Connection.* Teacher-learners, having taken the initial exploration, organization, identification, and classification steps, transfer new ideas from one teaching-learning situation to another. The teacher-learners experiment with taking parts out of a neat, sequential order of lesson plans and modifying, altering, and integrating ideas. Ready to use for designing thematic units and facilitating collaboration regarding new ideas, these professional design plans feature strategies, techniques, and concepts from other lessons and/or content areas.

- *Reflection.* The teacher and the teaching profession are one. Teachers often make informed decisions without conscious thought, intuitively reflecting and responding. Teacher-learners in the Learning Cycle Model are in a reflective action mode while teaching, having learned to listen to the student and respond. What teacher-learners do consciously as connectors, they do naturally as reflectors.

The rate and sequence that teacher-learners move through this cycle is dependent on prior experiences and the motivational energy invested in learning. Learning is dependent on how prior experiences relate to the current set of circumstances. Learning is situational or contextual; therefore, the process, the plan, and the learner needs vary from individual to individual and from situation to situation.

The teachers and their mentors/coaches or colleagues engage in a structured interview (see the next section for model interview questions), which helps identify their current repertoire of knowledge, skills, values, and attitudes in the context of their priority area for learning. They then can move to the Learner-Centered Coaching Model, in which the teacher-learner and coach identify the most appropriate type of support and mediation for learning.

The Learner-Centered Coaching Model

Developing teachers need support, an infusion of knowledge, and opportunities to integrate learnings. They are dependent on their work (their colleagues, their students, and themselves) to provide the feedback necessary to become continual learners in their profession. The Learner-Centered Coaching Model is designed to assist these teacher-learners and their mentor/coaches, peers, or supervisors in determining where they are in their learning cycle, as well as what coaching behaviors would be most effective in facilitating continuous learning.

For learning to take place, several factors must be considered. The factors that influence learning are

- Psychosocial/emotional development and well-being
- Experiential background—what has been observed and experienced
- Cognitive development—one's level of conceptual understanding and knowledge base

These factors form a *learner profile* or "frame of reference" for an individual, profiling the interaction with the teacher's learning environment, which consists of (1) the cognitive demands of the learning situation; (2) the potential for emotional and/or aesthetic response; and (3) the organization or structure for learning. This *learning environment* provides the "context" or "situation" for development.

How the Learner-Centered Coaching Model Works

The Learner-Centered Coaching Model helps the coach (mentor) and teacher-learner collaborate to determine their needs in the professional growth process. The coach and the teacher-learner can then decide on the most effective coaching role or style for building the competence and commitment of the teacher. Using appropriate guidance and support should lead to teacher autonomy and efficacy.

Key contributors to determining where the learner is in terms of his or her learning cycle are

- Levels of competence (experience and ability)
- Commitment (enthusiasm and willingness) in regard to the priority area for learning

These key contributors should be explored in the context of factors that form the learner profile and learning environment. In the context of learning priority, these contributors can be determined by asking questions aimed at identifying the current knowledge, skills, values, and attitudes of the teacher-learners.

Suggested Interview Questions

The interviewer should supply the individual's selected portfolio priority or focus (represented by the blanks) as he or she poses these questions:

1. Describe how you _____.
2. How do you know if _____ is working?
3. What have you heard about or seen in regard to _____ that you would like to try?
4. What would you like to do, or do differently, as far as _____ is concerned?
5. How do you feel about where you are _____?

After exploring the individual's knowledge, skills, attitudes, and values, the teacher-learner, together with the coach, can decide where they are in their cycle and develop an appropriate learning plan. The level of direction for developing and implementing the plan can be determined by learning needs, facilitated by the portfolio process.

The coaches, peers, and/or supervisors can define their roles in response to the teacher-learner needs. The roles for coaching or guidance are advisor, planner, collaborator, and resource person.

- *Advisor:* This role is compatible with learners who are in the *explorer* phase of their cycle. They are beginning to discover, identify, observe, and gather experiences that will help them identify a priority for learning. The mentor/coach offers support and direction by making suggestions for discovery and exploration activities. He or she helps the teacher-learner identify and clarify issues that have emerged from experiences and observations.

- *Planner:* This role is compatible with teacher-learners who are moving into the *organization* phase of their learning cycle. They are starting to focus and identify a specific area for learning. As the teachers learn the terms, techniques, and successful practices related to their identified priority, the mentor/coaches help them clarify their focus and build a plan for organizing and implementing their learnings.

- *Collaborator:* This role is compatible with teacher-learners who are in the *connection* phase of their learning cycle. They have tried new practices and are at the point where they begin to modify, adapt, and transfer learnings into other areas of their professional practice. The mentor/coach works side-by-side with the teacher in planning, observing, implementing, and adapting new practices. Often new ideas and suggestions emerge from these two-way, collaborative conversations.

- *Resource person:* This role is compatible with teacher-learners who are at the *reflection* phase of their learning cycle, that is, in a targeted area of learning. Teacher-learners have internalized new ideas and made decisions to use these new practices while actively teaching. The coach is a resource, available for support, guidance, or feedback when the teacher calls for it.

All four roles enlist varying measures of support and direction based on learner needs. Thus, the proper amount of psychological support, direc-

tion, and knowledge-building experiences necessary to assist the teacher can be identified. Coaches or mentors continually adapt their roles in the learning process to match the needs of the teacher-learners. This methodology facilitates continuous learning and reflection on learnings. Providing closure in the inquiry process as the learner completes the cycle, the Learner-Centered Coaching Model facilitates the professional development portfolio process and identifies a new priority for learning.

Summary

The Learner-Centered Coaching Model has been used successfully with both beginning and veteran teachers. The following benefits have been observed:

1. Focused learning—allowing for deeper levels of understanding

2. Alignment between the individual teacher's goals and those of the school

3. Clear definition of the role of coach, peer, mentor, or supervisor

4. Transfer of "learning-to-learn" principles to the classroom

5. Increased impact of professional development activities

6. Contribution to building a collegial culture in the school community

7. Practicing of collaboration techniques

8. Eagerness to learn from experiences

9. Integration of learning and assessment models (best practices) in the classroom.

Glossary

Bibliography

Index

Glossary

action research. Educators researching in schools settings. Learning community members pose questions regarding their practice, focusing their inquiry through their daily practices. In action research, teachers draw questions from the classroom or from dilemmas that exist beyond the classroom door. The power of collaboration and reflection enhances the connections between classroom practices and research.

artifact registry. Part of the structured journal where the teacher records the artifacts and evidence compiled in the portfolio, keeping track if, when, and why they are removed.

artifacts. In terms of the portfolio and the journaling process, items that reflect who you are, what you do, what is important to you, and what your major interests are.

change facilitation. The process of building capacity for having conversations that assist in forming attitudes and establishing norms, which support members of a learning community through the transitions of change.

checkpoints. Features of the portfolio process, such as artifacts and evidences, partner meetings, individual induction plans, activities, and professional credo. These points serve as catalysts for discussion (and journaling) about the progress and success of the portfolio process.

co-evolving systems. Recognition of the interdependence of actions, attitudes, and the establishment of structures in a system. There are long-term and short-term influences as well as effects of actions on the system. The system is always in the process of evolving (changing/becoming) as are the participants in the system.

collaborations. The group processes in which school community members participate during the school term; for example, study groups, seminars, peer coaching groups, and the sharing of experiences and learnings by professional portfolio users.

collegial collaborations.   Conversations, reflections, dialogues, and decision making that involve deep levels of understanding, commitment, reflection, and honesty; collaborations where assumptions are suspended and intentions articulated. The purpose for the collaboration invites questioning practices and construction of new understandings.

community.   A collection of individuals with a shared purpose in a climate of caring; an environment in which open communication, interdependence, and reciprocal processes are accepted as the norm.

constructivism.   The theory that knowledge should be *constructed* by the learner rather than being transferred from the teacher to the learner; a way to make meaning by interfacing with people, objects, and ideas.

constructivist leadership.   The reciprocal process which enables participants in an educational community to construct meanings which lead toward a common purpose about schooling (Lambert 1995, 29).

constructivist teaching.   A teaching methodology that focuses on creating environments where learners can discover, construct, invent, and restructure knowledge. Simply put, if learning is knowledge constructed through experiences, then constructivist teaching facilitates the learning process through experiences.

contributors.   In the context of frameworks for change, smaller ideas that require more detailed consideration, and emerge through the inquiry process of perusing a priority for learning.

credo.   A statement that reflects a current belief system.

disequilibrium.   In a learning community, an instance when the learner begins to sense contradictions in community members' reasoning or in existing structures; when ideas break down and then, ideally, are eventually reorganized into new thought patterns and structures.

evaluation.   An assessment of a process to find out if that process is serving its identified purpose. Ideally, measurements that determine success can be agreed upon—from the beginning—by all of those involved in the process.

evidence.   A document or documents that represent the educator's current level of expertise and professional engagement; evidence may include credentials, letters of recommendation, students' work, etc.

feedback.   Information provided to another about what he or she has said or done. This information helps to clarify and respond to what has been observed or heard.

frame of reference.   The multiple perspectives that contribute to one's perception of what is, and the understanding of people, events, ideas, and actions. The frame of reference is based on the individual's experiences, histories, knowledge base, and capacity to listen and learn.

individual learning plan.   A design that contains activities, goals, and development suggestions to support and assist the teacher.

instructional practices.   The strategies, techniques, and processes teachers employ in facilitating learning with their students.

journal.   In the context of frameworks for change, a process designed to guide teachers as they participate in learning communities, as well as build and implement their professional development plans (portfolios). The process features opportunities for structured journal entries and recording of reflections, observations, and learnings—designed to share with peers, supervisors, and other community members.

learner portfolio.   An "envelope of the mind" containing a collection of artifacts and evidence that represent the current level of performance of the learner. The purpose is identified by the teacher-learner and influences the structure and process for the portfolio.

learning community.   A reference to the processes and relationships among group members that enable the entire community to learn and change. These processes and relationships include inquiry, dialogue, reflection, and action.

Learning Cycle Model.   Designed for professional learning, a process for determining appropriate learning activities in order to construct new and deeper understandings (see Appendix).

learning organization.   An organization comprised of learning communities; communities where members are adaptive, generative, and creative learners. Groups of individuals who have come together with a shared purpose and agree to construct new understandings. . . "a place where people continually expand their capacity to create the results they truly desire, where new and expansive patterns of thinking are nurtured, where collective aspiration is set free, and where people are continually learning how to learn together" (Senge 1990, 24).

living systems.   Systems that include living organisms, contributors to the function, maintenance, and evolution of the system and its members. A living system has the ability to adapt, restructure, evolve, reform, and regenerate contributors and members of the system.

mechanistic system.   A system that is machine-like, hierarchical, and designed to preserve the status quo.

mental maps.   The collection of ideas, experiences, and emotional development of an individual, which all contribute to the structures called upon to interpret and perceive events, information, and new ideas. Sometimes referred to as *frame of reference* or *point of view.*

modify.   To alter, adapt, or change a process or design in order to better serve the agreed upon purpose.

partner meeting.   In the professional growth framework, an opportunity for the teacher to meet with his or her partner and (1) share entries and deletions in the artifact registry; (2) discuss current professional development activities; 3) update the professional portfolio priority/focus; and (4) collaborate regarding progress and possible modifications in the individual learning plan.

peer coaching.   Pairs of teachers taking turns observing each other for the purpose of planning, designing, and refining their curriculum and instructional practices; also, a confidential process through which teachers share their expertise and provide one another with feedback, support, and assistance for the purpose of refining present skills, learning new skills, and/or solving classroom-related issues.

point of view.   The perception in one's frame of reference or mental model for perceiving and interacting. It influences the assumptions individuals make about their own intentions and actions as well as those of others.

portfolio partner.   In the professional growth framework, a colleague with whom the portfolio user meets on a regular basis, in order to share and reflect on items in the portfolio as well as activities in the professional development plan.

portfolio priority.   An essential theme or focus in the professional portfolio process; a special interest or concern that the portfolio user has in terms of instructional practices and student outcomes; for example, class structure, grouping students effectively, variations for lesson designs, or block scheduling.

professional communities.   In the larger school community, those groups that primarily concern educators in their shared work of professional development.

professional development activities.   Learning opportunities that are included in the teacher's individual learning plan; for example, a course at a local university, staff development sessions at school, seminars that fit into the plan, observations of others' teaching, peer coaching participation, or selected professional readings (books/articles).

Professional Development Cycle.   A model for identifying patterns of teacher development; a guide to identify where a teacher might be in the career cycle and what he or she need to do to keep on growing as a professional (see Appendix).

professional development plan.   A collection of activities that relate to the teacher's focus for learning and to the general (schoolwide) goals for the school.

professional growth portfolio.   A process (framework for change) that provides educators with a structure or "cognitive tool" for initiating, planning, and facilitating personal/professional growth, while building connections between their personal interests and goals and those of the school.

professional teachers.   Those committed to first doing no harm; educators who continually seek more effective practices and revisit their purposes for schooling. Professional teachers facilitate learning for their students, honoring the individual's point of view and posing questions to help students find relevance to their learning. Professional teachers engage in "acts of leadership" at many levels in the school system and are committed to building community.

relationships.   The interactions that inform individuals as to who they are and contribute to forming purpose and meaning in life. Relationships can provide support and caring in a community or they can be destructive and painful, depending on the varying contexts (home, school, etc.) and individual needs, capacities, and fears.

school communities.   Those institutions or organizations with open boundaries of membership; including educators, children and their families, school board members, community leaders, local businesspeople, and other members of the larger community.

school portfolio.   A process (framework for change) used as a communication method to report on the status of school programs and student progress to the community at large; also used as a way to celebrate accomplishments and plan for the future. A flexible tool, the portfolio can be used as part of the process schools go through as they apply for educational grants.

study group.   A framework for change; a collection of individuals who share a common interest or need for inquiry. The study group participants make a commitment to work together to support their colleagues' learning, forming effective collaborations along the inquiry path. Often a study group in a school community forms to read and reflect on a professional/educational book that includes information pertinent to the group members, or one that reflects a shared interest.

zone of proximal development.   The area in which one can learn with the support and/or mediation of a mediator or fellow learner; often referred to as one's instructional level, "entry point," or zone for learning (Vygotsky 1962).

Bibliography

Airasian, Peter W., and Arlen R. Gullickson. *Teacher Self-Evaluation Kit.* Thousand Oaks, CA: Corwin Press, Inc., 1997.

Apple, Michael, and James Beane. *Democratic Schools.* Alexandria, VA: Association for Supervision and Curriculum Development, 1995.

Armstrong, Thomas. *Multiple Intelligences in the Classroom.* Alexandria, VA: Association for Supervision and Curriculum Development, 1994.

Bailey, Suzanne. "Structured Dialogue: Inserting New Cultural Norms One Conversation at a Time." *Association for Supervision and Curriculum Development Presents: Satellite Broadcast with Suzanne Bailey—Part II* (videotape). Alexandria, VA: Association for Supervision and Curriculum Development, 1995.

———. *Facilitation in the 21st Century?* Danville, CA: Systems Guides Development Session, 1996.

Bernhardt, Victoria L. *The School Portfolio: A Comprehensive Framework for School Improvement.* Princeton Junction, NJ: Eye on Education, 1994.

Block, Peter. *Stewardship: Choosing Service Over Self-Interest.* San Francisco: Berrett-Koehler Publishers, 1993.

Braham, Barbara. *Finding Your Purpose: A Guide to Personal Fulfillment.* Menlo Park, CA: Crisp Publications, 1991.

Bridges, William. *Managing Transitions: Making the Most of Change.* Menlo Park, CA: Addison-Wesley Publishing, 1991.

Brooks, Jacqueline Grennon, and Martin Brooks. *In Search of Understanding: The Case for Constructivist Classrooms,* Association for Supervision and Curriculum Development, 1993.

Burke, Kay. *Designing Professional Portfolios for Change.* Arlington Heights, IL: IRI/SkyLight Training and Publishing, 1997.

———, ed. *Professional Portfolios: A Collection of Articles.* Arlington Heights, IL: IRI/SkyLight Training and Publishing, 1996.

Byham, William C. *Zapp in Education: How Empowerment Can Improve the Quality of Instruction, and Student and Teacher Satisfaction.* New York: Fawcett Books, 1992.

Canning, Christine. "What Teachers Say about Reflection." *Educational Leadership* (March 1991): 18-21.

Capra, Fritjof. *The Turning Point.* New York: Simon & Schuster, 1982.

Chawla, Sarita, and John Renesch, eds. *Learning Organizations: Developing Cultures for Tomorrow's Workplace.* Portland, OR: Productivity Press, 1994.

Churchland, Paul. *The Engine of Reason, the Seat of the Soul.* Cambridge, MA: The Massachusetts Institute of Technology Press, 1995.

Costa, Arthur, L. and Bena Kallick, eds. *Assessment in the Learning Organization: Shifting the Paradigm.* Alexandria, VA: Association for Supervision and Curriculum Development, 1995.

Covey, Stephen. *Principle-Centered Leadership.* Hamden, CT: Fireside Press, 1990.

Darling-Hammond, Linda. "Reframing the School Reform Agenda." *Phi Delta Kappan* (June 1993).

———. *Professional Development Schools: Schools for Developing a Profession.* New York: Teachers College Press, 1994.

———. "What Matters Most: A Competent Teacher for Every Child." *Phi Delta Kappan* 78, no. 3 (1996): 198–200.

Dietz, Mary E. *Professional Development Portfolio: A Site-Based Professional Development Program.* San Ramon, CA: Frameworks, 1991.

———. "Portfolio Power: A System for Professional Development of Teachers." Association for Supervision and Curriculum Development, *Human Resource Development Newsletter* (Fall 1992).

———. "Professional Development Portfolio: A Constructivist Approach to Teacher Development." Paper presented at the Annual Conference of Critical Thinking, Massachusetts Institute of Technology, Boston, 1993.

Dietz, Mary E., Nanette Green, and Judy Piper. *Facilitating Learning Communities: Facilitator's Manual.* Oxford, OH: National Staff Development Council, 1998.

Dolan, Patrick. *Restructuring Our Schools: A Primer on Systemic Change.* Kansas City, MO: Within Systems and Organization, 1994.

Edgerton, Russell, Pat Hutchings, and Kathleen Quinlan. *The Teaching Portfolio: Capturing the Scholarship in Teaching.* Washington, DC: American Association for Higher Education, 1991.

Fosnot, Catherine, T. *Learning to Teach, Teaching to Learn: Center for Constructivist Teaching/Teacher Preparation Project.* Paper presented at the Annual Conference of the American Educational Research Association, San Francisco, CA, 1992.

Fullan, Michael. *The New Meaning of Educational Change.* New York: Teachers College Press, 1991.

Gardner, Howard. *The Unschooled Mind.* New York: Basic Books, 1991.

Glasser, William. *The Quality School Teacher: A Companion Volume to Quality Schools.* New York: HarperCollins Publishers, 1993.

Glickman, Carl. *Supervision in Transition—1992 Yearbook of the Association for Supervision and Curriculum Development.* Alexandria, VA: Association for Supervision and Curriculum Development, 1992.

————. *Renewing America's Schools: A Guide for School Based Action.* San Francisco, CA: Jossey-Bass Publishers, 1993.

Graves, Sharon S. "An Examination of the Value of the Professional Development Portfolio: A Conceptual Framework for Professional Growth." Ph. D. diss., University of Ohio, June 1996.

Guskey, Thomas R. "Results-Oriented Professional Development: In Search of an Optimal Mix of Effective Practices." *Journal of Staff Development* (Fall 1994).

Hutchings, Pat. *Campus Use of the Teaching Portfolio, Twenty-Five Profiles.* Washington, DC: American Association for Higher Education, 1993.

Hyerle, David. *Visual Tools for Constructing Knowledge.* Alexandria, VA: Association for Supervision and Curriculum Development, 1996.

Jalongo, Mary Renck. *Creating Learning Communities: The Role of the Teacher in the 21st Century.* Bloomington, IN: National Educational Service, 1991.

Jensen, Eric. *The Brain-Based Approach.* Del Mar, CA: Turning Point Publishing, 1996.

Johnson, Margaret J., and Katherine Bulton. "Action Research Paves the Way for Continuing Improvement." *Journal of Staff Development* 19, no. 1 (November 1998): 48–51.

Joyce, Bruce. *Changing School Culture Through Staff Development.* Alexandria, VA: Association for Supervision and Curriculum Development, 1990.

Joyce, Bruce, James Wolf, and Emily Calhoun. *The Self-Renewing School.* Alexandria, VA: Association for Supervision and Curriculum Development, 1993.

Katzenmeyer, Marilyn, and Gayle Moller. *Awakening the Sleepy Giant, Leadership Development for Teachers.* Thousand Oaks, CA: Corwin Press, 1996.

Killion, Joellen P., and Guy R. Todnem. "A Process for Personal Theory Building. *Educational Leadership* (March 1991): 14-16.

Lambert, Linda, et al. *The Constructivist Leader.* New York: Teachers College Press, 1995.

———. *Who Will Save Our Schools: Teachers as Constructivist Leaders.* Thousand Oaks, CA: Corwin Press, 1996.

Lazear, David. *Seven Ways of Knowing: Teaching for Multiple Intelligences.* Arlington Heights, IL: IRI/ SkyLight Training and Publishing, 1991.

Levine, Marsha. *Professional Practice Schools: Linking Teacher Education and School Reform.* New York: Teachers College Press, 1992.

Lewis, Anne. *Restructuring America's Schools.* Arlington, VA: American Association of School Administrators, 1991.

Mamchur, Carolyn. *Cognitive Type Theory and Learning Style.* Alexandria, CA: Association for Supervision and Curriculum Development, 1996.

McCarthy, Kevin W. *The On-Purpose Person.* Colorado Springs, CO: Pinon Press, 1992.

McLaughlin, Maureen, and Mary Ellen Vogt. *Portfolios in Teacher Education.* Newark, DE: International Reading Association, 1996.

Millman, Jason, and Linda Darling-Hammond, eds. *The New Handbook of Teacher Evaluation: Assessing Elementary and Secondary School Teachers.* Newbury Park, CA: Corwin Press, 1996.

Moye, Valerie H. *Conditions That Support Transfer for Change.* Arlington Heights, IL: IRI/SkyLight Training and Publishing, 1997.

Murphy, Carlene. "Whole-Faculty Study Groups: Doing the Seemingly Undoable." *Journal of Staff Development* (Summer 1995): 35–40.

Owen, Jill, Pat Cox, and John Watkins. *Genuine Reward: Community Inquiry into Connecting Learning, Teaching, and Assessing.* Andover, MA: The Regional Laboratory, 1994.

Piaget, Jean. *The Development of Thought: Equilibration of Cognitive Structures.* New York: Viking Press, 1977.

Poplin, Mary. *Voices From the Inside: A Report on Schooling From Inside the Classroom.* Claremont, CA: The Institute for School, 1994.

Regional Laboratory for Educational Improvement for the North East and Islands. *Creating New Visions for Schools: Activities for Educators, Parents, and Community Members.* Andover, MA: Regional Laboratory for Educational Improvement for the North East and Islands, 1994.

Reiman, Allan J., and Lois Thies-Sprinthall. "Promoting the Development of Mentor Teachers: Theory and Research Programs Using Guided Reflection." *Journal of Research and Development in Education* 26, no. 3 (1993): 179–185.

Renyi, Judith. *Teachers Take Charge of Their Learning: Transforming Professional Development for Student Success.* Washington, DC: National Foundation for the Improvement of Education, 1996.

Rosenholtz, Susan J. *Teachers' Workplace: The Social Organization of Schools.* New York: Teachers College Press, 1991.

Sagor, Richard. *Collaborative Action Research.* Washington, DC: Association for Supervision and Curriculum Development, 1990.

Schmoker, Mike. *Results: The Key to Continuous School Improvement.* Alexandria, VA: Association for Supervision and Curriculum Development, 1996.

Schmuck, Richard A. *Practical Action Research for Change.* Arlington Heights, IL: IRI/SkyLight Training and Publishing, 1997.

Senge, Peter M. *The Fifth Discipline: The Art and Practice of the Learning Organization.* New York: Doubleday, 1990.

———. *The Fifth Discipline: Field Book.* New York: Doubleday, 1994.

———. "The Tragedy of Our Times." In *Systems Thinking Basics: From Concepts to Causual Loops,* edited by Virginia Anderson and Lauren Johnson. Waltham, MA: Pegasus Communications, 1997.

Sergiovanni, Thomas J. *Building Community in Schools.* San Francisco, CA: Jossey-Bass Publishers, 1994.

Vygotsky, Lev S. *Thought and Language.* Cambridge, MA: MIT Press, 1962.

———. *Mind in Society.* Cambridge, MA: Harvard University Press, 1978.

Wheatley, Margaret J. *Leadership and the New Science.* San Francisco, CA: Berrett-Koehler Publishers, 1992.

Whitmore, John. *Coaching for Performance.* Sonoma, CA: Nicholas Brealey Publishing Limited, 1996.

Wolf, Kenneth, and Mary Dietz. "Teaching Portfolios: Purposes and Possibilities." *Teacher Education Quarterly* 25, no. 1, 1998: 9–22.

Zemelman, Steven, Harvey Daniels, and Arthur Hyde. *Best Practice: New Standards for Teaching and Learning in America's Schools.* Portsmouth, NH: Heinemann, 1993.

Index

Action Priority Wheel, 50, 53, 116, 117
Action research, 1, 11, 13, 135
    as learning opportunity for teachers, 13
    background of, 13–14
    identifying opportunities for using, 24
    impact on teaching practices, 13
    wrap-up for, 23
Action research groups
    participation in, 14
    purpose statement for, 16, 90
Action research journal, 13–24
    case study on, 16–22
    focus of, 15, 18–19, 91–92
    organization of, 14–15
    outcome of, 15–16. 22, 96–97
    process of, 15, 19–22, 93–95
    purpose of, 15, 16–18, 89–90
    using, 14–16
Action teams, 9
Advisors, 131
Artifacts, 27, 36, 135
    collecting, 98
    in school portfolio, 53
Artifacts and evidence registry, 56, 107, 120, 135
Assessment, 64

Banner questions, 18, 28, 33–33, 71–72, 91, 102
Block scheduling, 7
Block, Peter, 7
Brain-compatible learning, 60
Brainstorming, 84
Building relationships, importance of, 9–10

Carousel, 78
Central Union High School (El Centro, CA), 26
Change facilitation, 135
Checkpoint dates, 34
Checkpoint meeting, 28
Checkpoints, 64, 65, 135
Children, uniqueness of, 6–7
Clark, Christopher, 25–26
Class-size reduction, 14
Co-evolving systems, 7, 135
Co-learning as reciprocal process, 9
Cognitive development, 131
Collaborations, 36, 106, 135
    collegial, 136
    in staff development, 3
    purposes of, 69
Collegial conversations, 9
Collegial development, 30, 99

Collegial sharing, 3
Collegiality, 10
Community, 136
Connection in Learning Cycle Model, 130, 132
Conscious listening, 80
Constructive controversy, 79
Constructivism, 136
Constructivist approach to teacher development, 129
Constructivist collaboration, 69–70
Constructivist leadership, 136
Constructivist teaching, 136
Consulting line, 78
Continuous learning, 43, 129, 130
Contributors, 136
Conversations, 8, 9
    collegial, 9
    critical friend, 70
    importance of, in building relationships, 9–10
    reflective, 70
    sharing and supporting, 70
Credo, 136
    defining your professional, 31, 100
Critical friend conversations, 70
Cut story, 78

Darling-Hammond, Linda, 42
Data collection, 21–22, 23, 95
Debriefing, 70
Dewey, John, 13
Discussion, 69
Disequilibrium, 136
Dyslexia, 6

Emotional development and well-being, 131
Entry points, 30, 31
Evaluation, 136
Evidence, 136. *See also* Artifacts and evidence registry
    collecting, 98
Experiential backgroun, 131
Exploration in Learning Cycle Model, 130, 131

Facilitation
    change, 135
    of learning communities, 1, 11–12
    strategies in, 78–79
    tools in, 54
Feedback, 136
Fish bowl, 79
Focus development, 98
Focused learning, 129–130, 132
Focusing, 18
Frame of reference, 136

Graves, Sharon, 27
Guskey, Thomas, 42

"How Will It Work" form as facilitation tool, 54

Individual learning plan, 136
Instructional practices, 136
Integrated curriculum design, 60
Isolation, 38

Jigsaw, 78
Journals, 136
    action research, 13–24
    professional growth, 25–39
    purpose of, 1
    role of, in building learning communities, 1–2
    school portfolio, 49–58
    staff development, 41–58
    study group, 59–66

Lead-ins, 19
Leadership
    abilities in, 99
    constructivist, 136
Learner portfolio, 74, 136
Learner-Centered Coaching Model, 129, 130–131
    application of, 131
    benefits of, 132
    interview questions for, 131–132
Learner-centered theories, 42
Learning
    continuous, 129, 130
    focused, 129–130
Learning centers, effectiveness of, 22
Learning communities, 1, 137
    attitudes and attributes of, 12
    building, in schools, 5–7, 14
    clusters of, 5
    essential qualities and roles of members, 10–11
    facilitating, 1, 11–12
    lack of, 5
    members of, 9
    nature of, 7
    need for, in schools, 7–8
    need to defind common purpose and function for, 10
    portfolio checklists for building, 73
    role of journals in building, 1–2
    thoughtul questions for, 81
Learning Cycle Model, 62, 129–130, 137
    connection in, 130, 132
    exploration in, 130, 131

organization in, 130, 132
    reflection in, 130, 132
Learning cycle of professional development, 129–132
Learning environment, 131
    creating, 6
Learning needs as learner-centered, 3
Learning opportunities
    defining, 30–31
    descriptions of, 31, 98–99
Learning organizations, 1, 5, 137
    nature of, 7
Learning plan, building and adapting, 30, 98
Learning theory, translation into professional development, 129
Learning-to-learn principles, 132
Listening, levels of, 80
Listener, role of, 77
Living systems, 137

Management skills, sharpening, 30, 98
Mechanistic system, 137
Mental maps, 137
Modify, 137
Multimedia metaphor, 78
Multiple intelligences, 60

National Board of Teaching Standards, 25
Need-to-dos, 32
New York City Teacher Center Consortium, 6, 26

Observations, 3, 90
Observer, role of, 77
Orange County (FL) Public Schools, 26
Organization in Learning Cycle Model, 130, 132

Partner meetings, 3, 137
Past experiences and knowledge, drawing on, 30, 99, 130
Peer coaching, 137
Peer collaborations, 3, 25, 30, 98
    purposes, processes, and outcomes of, 69–70
Peer-with-peer interaction, 3
Perceptual disability, 6
Planners, 132
Point of view, 137
Portfolio checkpoints, for building a learning community, 73
Portfolio development, stages of, 27
Portfolio partner, 137
Portfolio priority, 137
Presentation portfolio, 25, 74
Priorities, worksheet for defining, 82
Priority action team worksheet, 55, 119

Priority work group, 116
Professional collaboration, 14
    guide for, 69–70
Professional communities, 137
Professional development
    activities in, 3, 34, 104, 137
    background of, 25–27
    checklist for building a learning community, 73
    learning cycle of, 129–132
    log for, 35, 105
    plan for, 34, 103–104, 138
    portfolio for, 27
    purpose-oriented, 5
    results-oriented, 42
    task-oriented, 5
Professional Development Consortium, 25
Professional Development Cycle, 138
Professional growth
    background of, 25–27
    guide to reflection on, 75
    wrap-up, 38
Professional growth journal, 25–39
    case study on, 28–37
    focus of, 28, 32–34
    identifying opportunities for using, 39
    organization of, 28
    outcome in, 28, 37, 108
    process of, 28, 34–37, 103–107
    purpose of, 28, 29–32
    uses of, 27–28
Professional growth portfolio, 138
Professional learning, guiding principles for continuous, 3
Professional portfolios, 1, 26
    types and purposes of, 74
Professional teachers, 138
    essential attributes of, 6–7
Program quality review, 12
Psychosocial/emotional development and well-being, 131
Purpose, 89
    worksheet for defining, 82
Purpose-oriented professional development, 5

Reflection, 3
    in Learning Cycle Model, 130, 132
Reflective collaborations, 3
Reflective conversations, 70
Relationships, 138
Research plan, 20–21, 93, 94
Research target, 92
Research target area, establishing, 15
Research target form, 18–19

Resource person, 132
Results-oriented professional development, 42
Roundtable discussion groups, 70, 98
Rubric, 83

School change, strategy for determining top priorities
    for, 84–85
School communities, 1, 138
    problems in, 9–10
School portfolio journal
    case study on, 50–57
    focus of, 50, 53–54
    outcome, 50, 121122
    process in, 50, 55–56, 118–121
    purpose of, 50, 51–53
    using, 49–50, 58
School portfolios, 1, 26–27, 138
    artifacts for, 53
    background of, 49
    purpose of, 114–115
    survey on, 83
    wrap-up, 56–57
Schools
    building learning communities in, 5–7
    need for learning communities in, 7–8
Self-directed professional development of teachers, 26
Senge, Peter, 1
Sentence stems, 19
Sergiovanni, Tom, 5
Sharing conversations, 70
Site-based management, 7–8
Splinter questions, 33, 102
Staff development, 1
    background of, 41
    collaboration in, 3
    identifying opportunities for, 48
    wrap-up, 46–47
Staff development journal, 41–58
    case study on, 43–46
    focus of, 43, 45, 110
    organization of, 42
    outcome, 43, 46
    process of, 43, 45, 111
    purpose of, 42–43, 44, 109
    using, 41–43
Storyteller, role of, 77
Student learning
    impact of class-size reduction on, 14
    observations on, 17

Student Profile Checklist, 54, 76
Study group journal, 59–66
    case study on, 61–65
    focus of, 60, 62, 123
    organization of, 60
    outcome in, 61, 64–65, 126
    process of, 60–61, 63–64, 124–125
    purpose of, 60, 61–62
Study groups, 1, 12, 138
    background of, 59–66
    opportunities for using, 66
    wrap-up, 65
Supporting conversations, 70

Tame problems, 10
Task-oriented professional development, 5
Teacher Assessment Project (Stanford), 25
Teacher-learners
    connection by, 130
    exploration of, 130
    observations by, 130
    organization by, 130
    reflection by, 130
Teacher-researchers, communities of, 14
Teachers
    action research as learning opportunity for, 13
    as informed visionaries, 6
    commitment to education, 6
    constructivist approach to development of, 129
    self-directed professional development of, 26
Teaching practices, impact of action research on, 13
Team facilitators, 8
Think-pair-share, 79
Thinking-meaning-centered curriculum, 71
Triads, directions for coaching, 77
True, Mariam, 25

Venn diagram, 32
Visual dialogue, 79

Walk the talk, 79
Want-to-dos, 32
Wheatley, Margaret, 10
Wolf, Kenneth, 25
Working portfolio, 25, 74

Zone of proximal development, 138

SkyLight Training and Publishing Inc.

There are

one-story intellects,

two-story intellects, and three-story

intellects with skylights. All fact collectors, who

have no aim beyond their facts, are one-story men. Two-story men

compare, reason, generalize, using the labors of the fact collectors as

well as their own. Three-story men idealize, imagine,

predict—their best illumination comes from

above, through the skylight.

—Oliver Wendell

Holmes

SkyLight

Training and Publishing Inc.